Obama Does Globalistan

Pepe Escobar

NIMBLE BOOKS

NIMBLE BOOKS LLC

Nimble Books LLC
1521 Martha Avenue
Ann Arbor, MI, USA 48103
http://www.NimbleBooks.com
wfz@nimblebooks.com
+1.734-330-2593

Version 1.0; last saved 2009-01-27.

Printed in the United States of America

ISBN-13: 978-1-934840-83-2
ISBN-10: 1-934840-83-1

Contents

NIMBLE BOOKS LLC

ABOUT THE AUTHOR

Pepe Escobar, born in Brazil in 1954, is the roving correspondent for Hong Kong/Thailand-based Asia Times (www.atimes.com) and analyst for Toronto/Washington-based The Real News (www.therealnews.com).

He has lived and worked as a foreign correspondent in London, Paris, Milan, Los Angeles and Singapore/Bangkok. Since 9/11 he has extensively covered Pakistan, Afghanistan, Central Asia, Iran, Iraq and the wider Middle East. He is the author of *Globalistan: How the Globalized World is Dissolving into Liquid War* (Nimble Books, 2007) and *Red Zone Blues: a Snapshot of Baghdad during the Surge* (Nimble Books, 2007). He was contributing editor to *The Empire and the Crescent* (Amal Books, Bristol), *Tutto in Vendita* (Nuovi Mondi Media, Italy) and *Shia Power: Next Target Iran?* (Vallentine Mitchell, London) and is associated with the new, Paris-based European Academy of Geopolitics. When not on the road, he lives between Sao Paulo, Washington and Bangkok.

Introduction: The Shock of the New

Ideals have strange attributes, among them changing into their opposite when scrupulously followed.

—*Robert Musil*

This essay was put together during—almost literally—a vacuum, a dreaded wasteland between frantically checking up on RealClearPolitics and FiveThirtyEight.com every fifteen minutes for the latest polls and a Lincolnesque inauguration in a wintry New Rome. Unlike grandiloquent U.S. corporate media exercises on how President Barack Obama will fix the world, it concerns a few key facts, chief among them how Obama will position himself in the Eurasian chessboard—the new New Great Game.

This essay is a companion to my own *Globalistan*, published in early 2007, which I defined as a warped geopolitical travel book. I argued then that in a context of re-medievalization—the world fragmented into "stans"—we are now living an intestinal war, an undeclared global civil war. Borrowing from Zygmunt Bauman's concept of liquid modernity, I called it Liquid War—and not only because of the global scramble for "black gold" oil and "blue gold" gas.

Globalistan was essentially a long reportage crisscrossing the world. This text reflects the fact that I spent most of 2008 in the U.S. following the presidential campaign. As far as New Rome is concerned, I'm usually outside looking in—the point of view of my dying profession, the foreign correspondent. In this text I'm most of the time inside looking out. *Globalistan* can be read as an on the ground—and underground - report on the Bush administration wasteland. This text could be something of a last chapter—out of the belly of the beast.

2009 is the Mother of all celebratory years. The 20 years of the fall of the Berlin Wall. The 30 years of the Iranian Islamic revolution. The 50 years of the Cuban revolution. The 60 years of NATO. The 70 years of World War II. The 80 years of the Great Depression. The 90 years of the Versailles Treaty. It's as if the world was turning on its gyre as in a psychedelic kaleidoscope reviving modern history in high-speed. And which figure

1

comes out of the kaleidoscope, grinning his cool, calm and collected best to deal with a 1929-style crisis, the new Cold War or perhaps to conduct Versailles-style diplomacy? Barack Hussein Obama.

It will be a bumpy ride. Nevertheless a few certainties already emerge.

This cannot be Empire—of the "we create our own reality" kind (as a Bush adviser told *The New York Times* in October 2004). Not anymore.

George W. Bush foolishly believed the hyperpower was entitled to a throne way up above from which it would dictate to the rest of the world. But already in 2003, one year after publishing his groundbreaking *Après l'Empire*, where he argued that the American system had become a problem instead of a solution to the world, and as U.S. corporate media was telling everyone to "get used" to American Empire, French geo-scholar Emmanuel Todd had laid down the law:

> *"The U.S. leadership doesn't know anymore where to turn. They know that they are monetarily dependant on the rest of the world, and they are afraid of becoming inconsequential. There are no more Nazis and Communists. While a demographic, democratic, and politically stabilizing world recognizes that it is increasingly less dependent on the U.S., America is discovering that it is increasingly dependent on the rest of the world. That is the reason for the rush into military action and adventures. It is classic."*

Another certainty: the Bush wasteland years proved the world is not flat. It is flat only if seen from a flatliner's business-class-limo-to-the-five-star-hotel perspective. And conducted by U.S. gun power plus soft power, this "flatness" lasted, in historical terms, for a few minutes only. The missionary lyricism that offers America as a benign leader of this flatness— riding on the waves of messianic Puritanism—fools no one: it is now overwhelmingly identified as just an imperialist mask.

After the Promethean evisceration of the world economy the *pensée unique* hysteric phase of deconstruction of the nation-state is also over. The middle classes—the main engine of the market economy—have been plunged back into precariousness, which they thought was a thing of the past when they detached themselves from the working classes.

Obama "inherits" a Globalistan where teeming masses have discovered, to their grief, that markets do not suppress poverty, unemployment and exploitation. The real Globalistan is a Babel Tower where nations, mercenary peoples, terrorists, democracies, dictatorships, tribes, nomad mafias and religious outfits fight for wealth, faith, land and liberty.

Gramsci would tell us that the old order is dead but the new one has not yet been born. Yeats would tell us "the center cannot hold." The only alternative to "anarchy loosened upon the world" now seems to be a multipolarity shared by the bigger powers and, Italian geostrategists would say, "lesser non-powers."

It was not Osama "dead or alive" bin Laden who almost broke America down. It was George W. Bush. It was not "Islamo-fascism" that almost broke America down. It was Wall Street greed and corruption. Talk about the enemy within.

Obama's key challenge may be that the U.S. ruling class, in these past three decades, has ended up believing in its own propaganda. Not only in the free market hysteria, but also in the idea that wars in the Middle East/Central Asia can be won in a few weeks.

But this goes way beyond a mere U.S. crisis. In an October 2008 interview to *Le Monde*, Immanuel Wallerstein, Yale's finest, once again stressed that in these past 30 years we have entered "the terminal phase of the capitalist system." As Wallerstein has extensively analyzed it, the economic development of East Asia, India, Latin America, "constitutes an insurmountable challenge to the 'world-economy' created by the West, which does not control the costs of accumulation anymore." In fact, says Wallerstein, the last 30 year-period of real accumulation has been possible only "because the Keynesian states joined their forces in the service of Capital."

Minimalist pragmatist Obama, for his part, knows he cannot go for radical reform in a country paralyzed by the rhetoric of the pioneer/rugged intrepid entrepreneur who wins on his own against all odds. This ideology worked wonders in the 19th century—when the matter was to conquer the Midwest and the Far West and force these regions to prosper under capitalist rules. Now, in post-modernity, the name of the game is social atomization. Politically—and after the Bush/Cheney system almost broke America down—the question is how Obama can come up with a great 21st century collective project.

A few days before Obama's inauguration something quite astonishing happened in Paris—like a gathering of 20th century revolutionaries. But the names of these revolutionaries were Tony Blair, Nicolas Sarkozy, Angela Merkel, Italy's minister of Economy Guido Tremonti, along with some of the world's top economists. And what were they denouncing? The horrors of speculative capitalism, the irresponsible greed of bankers, the intolerable misery of the poorest countries in the world, the dramatic impoverishment of middle classes all over the spectrum, the ugly face of globalization out of control. In other words: Globalistan, the real—not flat—almost ungovernable world.

Also a few days before Obama's inauguration I was walking the dark, wet streets of a wintry Rome—thinking about what new games would soon be unraveling in the New Rome. The temptation was to draw a parallel with the fall of the Roman Empire, overrun by barbarian vandals and visigoths—the new Rome, in the 21st century, overrun by civil unrest, barbarism inside the gates. Wallerstein believes that in 30 or 40 years a new system will have emerged. It could be a more egalitarian and redistributive system, or a system of exploitation even more violent than capitalism.

Those Roman ruins that mesmerized Freud and helped him to understand the layers of our unconscious in the end had a soothing effect. Instead of succumbing to nihilism, in the end I settled for the image of Obama as an Angelus Novus, not a decadent Roman emperor but perhaps a new, post-everything Medici, a New Renaissance prince. He spent months in that interminable campaign stressing "The time is now." Well, it certainly is. If, of course, New Rome's conniving courtiers won't stab him in the back.

—Rome, January 2009

1: Is it the Messiah? Or is it emperor Barack?

If you are a prisoner of the dream of the Other, you are damned.

Gilles Deleuze

All through the interminable 21 months of Barack Obama's self-described "improbable" race to the White House, not only press/politico chattering classes, Beltway insiders and outsiders and the sprawling netroots but the whole United States grappled with the Shakespearean question of his true identity. Thus Obama was a Muslim, a Marxist, a liberal, a vapid celebrity, an ivory-tower Ivy Leaguer, a crooked Chicago politician, a *madrassa*-made radical, a terrorist, an East Coast elitist, a foreigner, a con-man, a populist, a lackey of Wall Street speculators, armchair warriors, zealous Zionists and corporate lawyers, and all of the above—usually at the same time.

Then came the apotheosis of November 4, 2008. And immediately afterwards a title signed, sealed, and delivered by the Beltway-—Obama the Pragmatist—as in his national security team "sharing my pragmatism about the use of power."

Pragmatism may be a made in America school of philosophy according to which truth emerges from test-drives in reality. Practical consequences of belief do matter; abstractions—as in shoving democracy to the Middle East via preemptive war—not that much. But above all, in Beltwayspeak, "pragmatic" is code for someone who's non-ideological and post-partisan.

Obama is not as much a pragmatist as a post-ideological minimalist. That in itself makes him an ideal subject of **deconstruction**.

After the epic 2008 campaign thick volumes of French theory could be produced about the dizzying social circulation of signs engendered by, or derived from, Obamania; its political use of quotations; its non-stop cultural production of concepts. Playing on Obama's now legendary rhetorical dexterity, we could examine how he engaged in Derridean "dissemination" of traces; how effective he was in undermining Foucault's microphysics of power; how he plunged his legions of admirers into Deleuze's "flows" and "connections" on plans of immanence; and how his presidency would be able to shatter Baudrillard's "hyperreal space" of endless simulations.

But maybe we should get lost in this "wilderness of mirrors" (copyright T.S. Eliot in *Gerontion*) only after Obama's first term, based on the record. For now, let's concentrate on a few hyperreal layers of America itself, and how Obama might be able, if at all, to smash through the wilderness of mirrors.

A sort of national consensus spanning the libertarian left, the entire far right/neo-con/Zio-con armchair warrior crowd, plus the free market Berkeley/Chicago/Harvard crowd, in unison, hailing Obama's election as a historic moment and his Cabinet appointments as "reassuring" cannot but be, well, a suspicious wilderness of mirrors.

Perhaps hardcore waves of Lacanian therapy would uncover what is buried deep down in Washington's collective psyche: that George W. Bush ultimately failed not in content—in ideology—but in form—his dogmatic, incompetent, "unsound" (shades of Kurtz in *Apocalypse Now*), even toxic methods. This is manifest anyway in the dominant post-election Washington narrative, which essentially veils a tremendous pressure for Obama to do what the ruling elites feels Bush should have done—regardless of the fact that a great deal of these basic policies were and remain extremely flawed.

So it's not about the failure of neo-cons and all that comes with it—the unabashed cronyism, the deregulatory obsession, the gutting of the U.S. Constitution and the Bill of Rights, the preemptive wars. It's only about the failure of "ideology." Now that should be fertile terrain for post-ideological Obama.

1A. MARX IS BACK

Formidable German poet Heinrich Heine, in the middle of the 19th century, was no less than prophetic: "These doctors in revolution and their implacably determined disciples are the only men alive in Germany, and the future belongs to them."

In the introduction to a new edition of Marx and Engels' *Communist Manifesto* stressing its contemporary relevance ("the world the *Manifesto* describes has in no way disappeared"), the indispensable geographer, anthropologist, and destroyer of neoliberalism David Harvey of the City University of New York gleefully observes: "The *Manifesto*'s prescient description of what we now call globalization (with its cognates of off-shoring and de-industrialization and global interdependence) suggests a certain continuity within the historical geography of capitalism from 1848 until today."

All that is solid melts into air. Obama as the last link in a continuum. Marx and Engels, gurus more now than ever. Not a bad counterpunch to the appalling arrogance of the neoliberal Right and the—now failed—consensus (or *penséee unique*, as the French memorably put it) according to which the market economy is the necessary condition for modern democracy and its eternal rule.

Commenting on the *Manifesto*, Harvey underlines how "one of its modest proposals for reform—the centralization of credit in the hands of the state—seems to be well on the way to realization." And he adds: "Why not take up some of the other equally modest but wholly sensible proposals—such as free (and good) education for all children in public schools; equal liability of all to labor; a heavy progressive or graduated income tax to rid ourselves of the appalling social and economic inequalities that now surround us?"

A Marx-centered debate may be a novelty in the U.S. but not in France and England, where since 2005 there have been hearty discussions on the thesis that the fall of the Soviet Union freed Marx from his heirs and finally revealed himself as the inspired prophet of capitalism, capable of anticipating our liquid modernity's blatant social inequalities. As for Latin America and the Middle East Marxism, in its myriad versions, has never ceased to seduce intellectuals and progressive politicians.

Hungarian philosopher Gáspár Miklós Tamás points to a common ground between Marx and Aristotle. Their work is both esoteric and exoteric—that is, one hardcore vision consumed only by the chosen few and another one more on the pop side. Tamás explains how "a confusion between the two has produced a serious problem: his historical theory, exclusively concerning capitalist (thus modern) society was transformed into general metaphysics. That's what produced the Soviet variant, dogmatic and positivist."

Thus the "real" Marx is only being known by now, in the 21st century. His British biographer Francis Wheen bets he will be "the most influent thinker of the 21st century" In 2005 Wheen helped to convince BBC listeners to elect Marx as "the greatest philosopher of all time."

Well, Karl was definitely wired. What he called "reserve industrial army" is back today not in Dickensian hoods in Europe but in every major hood in the globalized economy. And what he called "the social question"—that is, how to close the enormous gap between rich and poor, including inequalities in health, education and chances of "making it"—has not been solved by the industrialized West by any means; that's why an overwhelming proportion of the global masses perceive globalization as a redistribution of global wealth to the benefit of Corporatistan and selected barons of capital.

1B. FROM MARX TO BECK

For years, German sociologist Ulrich Beck has been stressing in his books the precariousness of the global financial system and the need for transnational regulation (we are reminded of Zygmunt Bauman: "Civilization is vulnerable; it always stays but one shock away from inferno.")

In an interview to Arno Widmann of the *Frankfurter Rundschau* newspaper, Beck gleefully underlines how "a good number of Anglo-Saxon *laissez-faire* partisans became ardent defenders of Chinese-style authoritarian capitalism. It's the world upside down!" That it is—with the added bonus of a historical irony: a welfare state for financial capital "while salaried workers only have the right to the neoliberal doctrine." Beck also does not fail to notice the "comic aspect" of the total triumph of finance capitalism being the key reason for it being dragged into an "existential crisis."

Beck points to the false idea "curiously present in both ideologies, neoliberal and neo-Marxist" according to which the economy should define the limits of an eternally submissive political power. But in these new times where Chinese, Russians and Arabs have become the West's creditors, how to change from one system to another?

The "nomad elites of global liquid modernity" (Bauman) may know that the Bush-style unilateral approach failed, but no one knows how fast the supposed European model of mutual understanding will gell (bureaucratic hordes in Brussels despair of it over their *steak frites*). As a committed Europeanist, Beck hopes the financial crisis may herald the emergence of a politically united Europe—open to the rest of the world. For the moment, this is way too subjective.

Much to the alarm of Washington elites what Beck really prefers to talk about is the possibility of no less than a revolution, though not the way we expect it to happen: "The threat does not come from an external enemy but from within, from the heart of the system. And everybody is concerned by this threat, which harbors a *cosmopolitical* dimension" (that's why in this case a rebranding of the system, characterized for the past three decades as savage neoliberalism, towards "benign" capitalism, is essential).

And that brings us to Beck's theme that "we cannot have a clear vision of our situation if we don't learn to see the world with the eyes of others."

It's virtually impossible, to say the least, for insular Washington elites to see the world with the eyes of others. The political center in the U.S. may have shifted, and mildly left positions (at least in the U.S., certainly not in Europe, much less in Latin America) are now part of a consensus.

But what is ultimately behind Obama's "change"? During the presidential campaign, "change" was packaged basically as higher taxes for the wealthy few, the end of the Iraq war and a national health care reform.

Under an Obama presidency it's fair to expect meaningful change in civil liberties, the environment, regulatory issues, race relations, and diplomatic protocols. It has always been a puzzle to Western Europeans how such mesmerizing fortunes could be spent on Pentagon games and the militarization of space when the healthcare system is so dismal and tens of millions of Americans survive on food stamps. Now *that* would be cause for non-stop revolutions in Europe.

But then, after Obama's Chicago acceptance speech, "change" mutated into "experience"—as in the serial appointment to top and minor government positions of mostly the usual suspects in seamless, perpetual rotation between Washington, Wall Street, the Federal Reserve and selected perches in Academia.

Thus re-appointing Robert Gates at the Pentagon, appointing on-the-record-war-hawk Hillary Rodham Clinton to the State Department and peppering the Cabinet with humanitarian neo-cons would be a **question of** "reassuring" the establishment—not a stark **contrast between Obama's** soaring campaign rhetoric and his in-command political choices.

The problem is—once again—"ideology" rearing its ugly head, now disguised as "pragmatism." Obama's star-studded foreign policy team in the Pentagon, State Dept., Justice Dept. and the basket of intelligence agencies may be ideologically inclined and genetically programmed to continue prosecuting the Bush/Clinton/Bush global "war on terror," or the Pentagon's Long War, or Liquid War, which translates in practice into a multi-layered war against any national resistance movement in the "arc of instability" from the Horn of Africa to Central Asia via the Middle East—from Hezbollah and Hamas to the Sadrists, with Iran, Syria, Afghanistan, Pakistan, Somalia, Sudan, Palestine and Iraq as prime targets of choice.

The icing on this geopolitical cake may have been provided by Dick "Angler" Cheney himself. On a December 16, 2008 interview to *ABC News*, he defended Shock and Awe on Iraq, Guantanamo, illegal wiretapping and waterboarding ("We don't do torture") with an absolute straight face. Then he praised Obama for keeping Gates ("excellent"), qualified General Jim Jones as a "very, very effective" National Security Advisor and defined

Obama's Secretary of State Hillary Clinton as "tough," "smart" and "just what President Obama needs."

As historian Nick Turse has excruciatingly detailed in *The Complex: How the Military Invades our Everyday Lives*, the new, hip, high-tech military-industrial complex has redefined itself; Turse calls it the "Military, Industrial, Technological, Entertainment, Scientific, Media, Intelligence Corporate Complex." In sum: the Pentagon rules, and has a virtual chokehold on the fabric of U.S. society. Mix it with what John Gray has observed in *Black Mass: Apocalyptic Religion and the Death of Utopia* about the "utopian engineering" Iraqi project: "The failure of the project has been ascribed to deficiencies in its execution and the recalcitrance of the Iraqi people rather than any defects in the project itself."

No wonder under these circumstances progressives of all stripes suspect brand Obama of being just about a clever rebranding of Empire—a temporary, carefully-packaged and market-researched-to-death deflection of the barely exploding rage of tens of millions of Americans; a Who-coined "Meet the new boss, same as the old boss" (as in *Won't Get Fooled Again*) to prevent direct revolutionary action or the rise of a new, truly representative, mass political movement.

1C. MELTDOWN

And then there's the economy—the tidal crisis waves battering the landscape since fateful September 29, 2008, when the Dow Jones average plunged a memorable 777.7 points. Amidst the current tsunami of corporate debt and scared-to-death credit markets, London-based GFC Economics predicted that by spring 2009, the U.S. could be facing more than 1 million layoffs every single month.

Things, of course, have to be kept in perspective. On December 9, 2008 the UN's Rome-based Food and Agriculture Organization (FAO), in its annual report on "food insecurity," announced that 963 million people were threatened by famine in 2008—40 million more than 2007. And the forecast for 2009 is even grimmer. Take it as a sad slideshow of the neoliberal dream.

In a succinct article on the January 2009 issue of *Vanity Fair* Columbia University professor and Nobel prize winner Joseph Stiglitz—who is not part of Obama's team—summed it all up: "The truth is most of the individual mistakes boil down to just one: a belief that markets are self-adjusting and that the role of government should be minimal." Stiglitz concludes that the embrace by America and much of the rest of the world of a "flawed economic philosophy," in fact an ideology, "made it inevitable that we would eventually arrive at the place we are today." The corollary was offered by *London Banker* in an essay that went wildly viral on the net: "The market has failed, and officialdom is collaborating in perpetuating that failure."

The fearless Nouriel Roubini, a.k.a. Dr. Doom, professor of economics at NYU's Stern School and a market fox who has predicted the crisis no less than 10 years ago, has been arguing that the worst is yet to come for the global economy—devastating job losses in the U.S., major social upheaval around the world. As Roubini plainly summed it up to *Fortune* magazine in late 2008: This is "the bursting of a huge leveraged-up credit bubble"; "there's no bottom to it"; it's a global recession; it's becoming worse; recovery in 2010 and 2011, if there is one, "is going to be so weak that it's going to feel like a recession"; people should stay away from the stock market, commodities and credit. The key advice would be all too familiar to Asians, but not to Americans: "You should preserve capital." America will have to get used not only to the collapse of the foundation of the American dream—auto industry, home loans, job security—but with a stark new reality: conspicuous consumption is now way uncool.

Talk about a wilderness of mirrors. The paradigm of free market has been smashed. Corporatistan begs for Keynesianism—but only for the wealthy. It is indeed a systemic crisis, as Roubini had been warning. But it goes way beyond; the crisis of food security, the environmental crisis, the energy crisis, the financial crisis, it's all interlocked. Without even having to resort to Marx and Engels, it's clear this is a crisis of the whole capitalist mode of production—and of its narrative that explains the world, and life as we know it, as a ruthless, non-stop war of conquest, defeats and limitless production. Liquid War—the Hobbesian liquid modernity scenario—is bound to get even more liquid.

Top economists have warned Obamanomics will fail if it chooses "continuity" and "stability" as defined by Wall Street. A "free market" where financial institutions are not allowed to go belly up is a chimera. As the system is rotten to the core, things might not get exactly better with an Obama team that includes certified champions of the deregulation, hysterical privatization and outsourcing that led to total market meltdown. The fear is of Timothy Geithner and Larry Summers effecting redistribution U.S.-style, where the top 1% wealthiest Americans in 2001 together owned more than twice as much as the bottom 80% of the population. In terms of financial wealth—excluding equity in owner-occupied housing—the top 1% owned more than four times the bottom 80%.

Obamanomics may end up revealing itself as a mix of Herbert Hoover economics, New Deal economics and Reaganomics: blind support for the monster, trillionnaire Wall Street bailout; a $1 trillion and counting job-creation stimulus package dictated by market imperatives—or the supreme mission to rescue U.S. capitalism—enveloping a lot of investment in public works; and the financing of the package through the remaining top banks and Wall Street. Nobody has a clue how will it actually work.

Obamanomics may also spell few if any compensation for a staggering 100 million heads of U.S. families swindled of at least $5 trillion in savings and pensions; no significant help for a countless mass who will perhaps become permanently unemployed; and no sustained bailout of threatened households.

Progressives have noted that very few members of Obama's economic team represent the interests of the American working classes—including the thoroughly devastated, productive industrial economy. So what will the U.S. working classes do—from France-style protest rallies to non-violent civil disobedience—as a counterpunch to the Masters of the Universe, political and economic, encroaching on Obama and influencing his Cabinet members and his economic agenda?

It's got to be a case of "Workers of the U.S., unite." It's clear anyway what the mad-as-hell U.S. working classes want. The list is, well, substantial.

It includes a universal health care system, certainly not as advanced as socialized medicine in selected countries in Europe (a single payer system like in Canada will do); transparency and accountability regarding the busted, crooked financial giants; the U.S. government buying threatened mortgages at their current, depreciated value, not at inflated face value (that will cost U.S. taxpayers a lot less); nationalizing Citigroup and other inevitably busted banks and then use them to loan to people at reasonable rates; nationalizing the Fed (as with most Central Banks around the world); regulating the money-creation power of commercial banks; going back to the more progressive, pre-Bush era taxation system; taxing tax capital gains at the same rate as wages and profits; shutting down offshore tax havens; restoring the estate tax; capping property tax that is excluded from taxable income; public financing of public works projects (the U.S. government should pay for them, not banks); real-life competitive bidding for all these projects (no "rebuilding" of Iraq or post-Katrina New Orleans, Bush-administration crony-style); ending the wars in Iraq and Afghanistan; downsizing the Pentagon; closing down the worldwide Empire of Bases; and allocating the resulting hundreds of billions of dollars to public spending.

In sum: the working masses want the end of an ideology, neoliberalism—whose sharpest pre and post-mortem critic has been David Harvey. Michael Hudson from the University of Missouri, author of *Super Imperialism*, has tellingly defined the wish list as "a small step back toward the progressive era of a century ago."

Instead, only four weeks before Obama's inauguration, what the whole U.S. was getting was what Michael Kosares—who has followed money markets through the prism of gold for over 35 years—wrote about at the *USA Gold* website: "We have talked about the Weimarization of America here for many years... The Fed has made known its intentions. The commitment to print and helicopter drop money, through the wild expanse of the U.S. economy and financial markets ... has now officially been launched."

F. William Engdahl, author of the seminal *A Century of War*, writing on Global Research, is quick to identify what will happen in the long run: "Once banks begin finally to lend again, perhaps in a year or so, that will flood the U.S. economy with liquidity in the midst of a deflationary depression. At that point or perhaps well before, the dollar will collapse as foreign holders of U.S. Treasury bonds and other assets run. That will not be pleasant as the result would be a sharp appreciation in the euro and a crippling effect on exports in Germany and elsewhere should the nations of the EU and other non-dollar countries such as Russia, OPEC members and, above all, China not have arranged a new zone of stabilization apart from the dollar."

So what's left for the Obama presidency? Engdahl: "The world faces the greatest financial and economic challenges in history in coming months. The incoming Obama Administration faces a choice of literally nationalizing the credit system to insure a flow of credit to the real economy over the next 5 to 10 years, or face an economic Armageddon that will make the 1930's appear a mild recession by comparison."

What's missing in all these horror movie scenarios is a compelling narrative of a new society—a new interpretation of the future capable of galvanizing global masses, a new world, a new society, a new utopia. It's simply not there. And that transcends the Obama phenomenon. The auspicious concatenation of circumstances that allowed the emergence of Obama will never be replicated: eight cataclysmic years of Bush/neo-con ideological disasters; the devastating speed and dimension of Wall Street's implosion; Obama's notable personal charisma. That's reality. Plus those staggering 13 million email addresses and 35,000 self-starting affinity groups on MyBarackObama.com that configure the goldmine of Obama's grassroots. Will a transcending vision flow through this network or— coerced by realpolitik imperatives—will it be lost in a wilderness of mirrors?

1D. THE WAR ON TERROR/LONG WAR/LIQUID WAR

Even eminent Eric Hobsbawm, writing in *On Empire*, was forced to confess: "Frankly, I can't make sense of what has happened in the United States since 9/11 that enabled a group of political crazies to realize long-held plans for an unaccompanied solo performance of world supremacy."

It has been documented to oblivion how the "political crazies" made a tragic mess of their solo act—while all the time blaming it all on "Islamo-fascism." As for Obama, for him to understand in detail what radical Islam is all about, few could be a better guide than Professor of European Thought at the London School of Economics John Gray, one of Europe's towering intellects: "Talk of 'Islamo-fascim' obscures the larger debts of Islamism to Western thought. It is not only fascists who have believed that violence can give birth to a new society. So did Lenin and Bakunin, and radical Islam could with equal accuracy be called Islamo-Leninism or Islamo-anarchism. However the closest affinity is with the illiberal theory of popular sovereignty expounded by Rousseau and applied by Robespierre in the French Terror, and radical Islam may be best described as Islamo-Jacobinism."

So much for fallacious "Islamo-fascism." Thus Islamo-Jacobinism, al-Qaeda style, is "a modern revolutionary ideology, but it is also a millenarian movement with Islamic roots." Yes, "we" in the West secreted it—as the modern West's formative role is "the faith that violence can save the world." As Gray points out, "totalitarian terror in the last century was part of a Western project of taking history by storm. The twenty-first century began with another attempt at this project, with the Right taking over from the Left as the vehicle of revolutionary change."

Gray would also clarify to Obama that "liberal democracy cannot be established in most of the countries of the Middle East. In much of the region the choice is between secular despotism and Islamist rule." U.S. foreign policy loves secular despots—from Egypt's Mubarak to Gulf sheikhs—like candy. Islamist rule has shades—from Hamas in Gaza to a more secularized Hezbollah in Lebanon. Iraq under al-Maliki is veering towards secular despotism, and not Islamism.

Gray notably describes the Iranian regime as "an Islamist version of Rousseau's illiberal dream" (he is absolutely correct: Ayatollah Khomeini was a voracious reader not only of Rousseau but Aristotle. Rousseau's Legislator evolved into the figure of the Supreme Leader under Khomeini's theory of *velayat-e-faqih* (the primacy of the jurisprudent).

So the Obama presidency should warm up to Gray's warning: "When the remaining authoritarian regimes in the Middle East are overthrown it is likely to be this type of democracy that will succeed them." Let it be known that "these countries will not be clones of any Western political system, and the idea that a 'new Middle East' is on the horizon that will accept the United States as a model of government is fantasy."

As Tariq Ali has stressed in *The Duel: Pakistan on the Flight Path of American Power*, al-Qaeda "does not pose any serious threat to U.S. power. It is not even remotely comparable to the anti-colonial national liberation movements that tormented Britain, France and the United States in Africa or Indochina during the last century." To make it clear, Obama might pose a question or two to his prized adviser Zbig Brzezinksi, under whose watch al-Qaeda's historical leadership was incubated in Wahhabi Saudi Arabia and Egypt and then mobilized to wage jihad against the Soviets in Afghanistan—Zbig's master plan to bleed the Soviet empire.

As far as Bush's nonsensical "war on terror" is concerned Gray's advice is deceptively simple: "Declaring war on the world is not a sensible way of dealing" with Islamist terrorism. This is a security problem rather than a strategic threat. It involves painstakingly slow police work that "requires support from their host communities."

So what to do next? Obama could supplement Gray with Olivier Roy, research director at the French National Center for Scientific Research (CNRS) and one of the world's top experts on political Islam.

In *The Politics of Chaos in the Middle East*, Roy demolishes the idea that there is a 'geostrategy of Islam' that would explain all the present conflicts. And he also debunks the vision of the Muslim world "at war with the West" as "a fantasy": "Most of the conflicts affecting the Middle East involve Muslims against Muslims."

Roy extensively describes "the three traumas of the Arab Middle East"; without understanding in full how they have molded the modern Arab psyche, it's impossible for any U.S. administration to be perceived as a fair player. The traumas are: "The collapse of the project to build a great Arab kingdom out of the ruins of the Ottoman Empire, as promised by the British"; the creation of the state of Israel, at the moment when Arab states were getting independent and were dreaming again of Arab unity; and the current erosion of Sunni political supremacy (there are only two solidly Sunni states in the Middle East: Saudi Arabia and Jordan, plus a few Emirates).

So what's happening now? "We are witnessing the Islamization of Arabism. The civilizational divide expressed by the Huntingtonian thesis of the clash of civilizations is more popular in the Middle East, not because it expresses a traditional cultural identity, but on the contrary a recasting of pan-Arabism into a Muslim religious identity. Hence the success of Salafism. The lack of a real political perspective to fulfill the pan-Arab as well as pan-Islamic dream has led to a reversion to conservative cultural and social values, which creates fertile ground for Salafism."

As for Salafi-jihadis a la al-Qaeda, Roy depicts them as "a deterritorialized, global organization," relatively aloof in relation to Middle East problems, "with no political roots in the Muslim populations," recruiting mainly "among the 'born again' in the fringes." In sum, a very loose, nomadic network with a strong *esprit de corps* (and nothing to do with guerrilla techniques a la General Giap in Vietnam).

The corollary: you simply can't combat nomads by conquering territory, as the Bush administration had been doing under the "war on terror." And on top of it it's all random. Roy recalls a significant meeting he had in November 2001 with then all-powerful *uber*-neo-con Paul Wolfowitz. As Wolfowitz bluntly told Roy, Afghanistan was a "distraction," the real target was Iraq. It's as if Roy had an epiphany revealing to him all the U.S. moves in the new New Great Game: "That said it all: the Americans intervened in Afghanistan purely for reasons of expediency, because Bin Laden was there. But they had no long-term vision for the

Afghanistan-Pakistan-Central Asia region. This was consistent with the fact that Afghanistan had never interested Washington except negatively: against the Soviets and then against Bin Laden." And that also explains why the proposed Obama/Pentagon surge in Afghanistan will fail.

A true "grand bargain" towards a solution would include the end of Pakistan as a U.S. satrapy—something totally unsustainable even in the short run: instead of "war on terror" Washington should encourage a true land reform in Pakistan; a radical downsizing of the Pakistani military; and a really functioning social infrastructure for the Pakistani masses (education, health care, cheap housing). It won't happen.

As Srinivasan Ramani from India's *Economic and Political Weekly* succinctly puts it, the radicalization of the Pakistani military under Bhutto and then Zia ul-Haq, "plus the constant U.S. intervention in Pakistan grooming up the army," ended up in the maddeningly complex and virtually unbreakable ISI-military-jihadi Gordian knot. Even if Obama were a post-everything reincarnation of Alexander the Great the knot would still be there. The only thing that Washington cares about is the Waziristans and the tribal areas. As Ramani stresses, this has given " a blind eye to the ISI's *ronin* work which in turn has mollycoddled other radical groups with focus on Kashmir"—such as Lashkar e-Tayiba.

Also part of a true "grand bargain," solutions would include the end of U.S. support to outright dictators and nasty autocrats across the board—from Mubarak and King Abdullah to the House of Saud and Gulf sheikhs. It won't happen.

Investigative historian Gareth Porter told *The Real News* why in a July 2008 interview: In the U.S. "the terms of any public discourse on national security are so heavily weighted in favor of the national security bureaucracies' point of view that the news media essentially carry only one side... There's no surprise that someone as intelligent and in many ways progressive as Obama ... is a captive of... the Cold War mentality, a mentality that begins with a set of assumptions that have very little to do with reality."

Porter spent months during the 2008 U.S. presidential campaign asking some of Obama's advisors "whether they would support a change of policy regarding the whole idea of occupying Muslim lands," just as a basic principle. "None of them would say yes to that." His conclusion is glum: "I think that it's probably impossible to change the system from the inside. That would require a President who's ready to go down in flames... the willingness to essentially defy his entire national security bureaucracy."

As Slavoj Zizek has stressed in *Iraq: the Borrowed Kettle*: "The focus should be on what actually transpires in our societies, on what kind of society is emerging here and now as the result of the 'war on terror'. The ultimate result of the war will be a change in our political order." The Bush/neo-con change in the U.S. political order has been devastating. A reversed change in mentality is unlikely to happen in the short to medium run. Bottom line: under the Obama presidency, the war on terror/Long War/Liquid War is likely a go.

1E. Iraq/Afghanistan

Munthather al-Zaidi, the 28-year-old Baghdadi correspondent for the independent, anti-occupation, anti-sectarian, Cairo-based *Al-Baghdadiya* satellite channel who on December 14, 2008 sent George W. Bush a "goodbye kiss from the Iraqi people" in the form of a flying pair of size 10s and instantly achieved folk hero status all over the Arab nation and across *the internets* (copyright Bush), with a simple, graphically impeccable gesture brought to a closure not only Bush's ultra-secretive last stop in Iraq (a press conference with sometime U.S. puppet Prime Minister Nouri al-Maliki) but managed to single-handedly sum up the whole Iraqi tragedy.

No wonder al-Zaidi, a secular socialist Shi'ite from Sadr City, and a progressive journalist who documented the horrible social "collateral damage" of U.S. "precision strikes" on civilian targets was dubbed "the new Saladin" across the Arab world—and beyond. Iranian ayatollah Ahmad Jannati heartily praised the "shoe intifada" at Tehran University, where the clerical leadership has been excoriating the American "Great Satan" for three decades non-stop.

From now on three historic images will forever sum up the Bush administration-generated Iraqi tragedy: Bush's "Mission Accomplished" stunt off San Diego harbor; the "black scarecrow" figure tortured at Abu Ghraib; and Iraq's leather-soled kiss to the man who destroyed the country, dubbed by many *Sock and Awe*. The toppling of Saddam's statue in Baghdad's Firdous Square in April 9, 2003 was nothing but a staged event for U.S. networks.

Al-Zaidi called Bush, in Arabic, at the top of his lungs, *ya kalb* ("you dog")—a now legendary Youtube epithet that around the world was largely interpreted as unfair to dogs, who for all their barking do not gang up and launch preemptive wars that cause, directly and indirectly, more than 1 million deaths and displace more than 4 million people.

Before being brutally taken down by U.S. and Iraqi Secret Service ops, al-Zaidi still had time to yell "This is from the widows, the orphans and those who were killed in Iraq"—a factual, moving journalistic response to the lies he had just endured from Bush, who in his prepared remarks pontificated on the "success" of the Parliament-approved Status of Forces Agreement (SOFA), a "success' Bush attributed to the surge in Iraq.

For the record: the SOFA, negotiated after an extremely turbulent 8 months, rules the U.S. military must totally withdraw from Iraq by December 2011 (a real timeline, always fought by the Bush camp); there will be no remnants of the Empire of Bases left behind; and the U.S. military cannot use Iraq to attack Iran or anyone else. In theory the neocolonial Bush war/occupation will be over by the end of 2011 (Bush's White House was so exultant with this "success" that it did not even publish a copy of the SOFA in English).

In practice the Pentagon will move Himalayas and Hindu Kushes to Mesopotamia and relentlessly press Obama to thwart the agreement. The Pentagon's Gates could not be more explicit in a mid-December 2008 interview to Charlie Rose: "My guess is that you're looking at perhaps several tens of thousands of American troops, but clearly, in a very different role than we have played for the last five years."

University of Michigan professor Juan Cole, at his *Informed Comment* blog, gave plenty of reasons why this may be yet another recipe for disaster.

U.S. withdrawal by the end of 2011 is the "maximum" schedule Iraqi politicians and Grand Ayatollah Sistani will put up with and "the U.S. military cannot stay in Iraq against the will of the elected government"; Sistani—whose *fatwas* "must be obeyed by all adult Shi'ites who follow him (the majority of Iraq) will never allow it; the Sadrists will fight it to death; the Islamic Supreme Council of Iraq (ISCI), part of the government, along with their Iranian-trained Badr Corps will never accept it because "they want to assert control over Iraq themselves"; the Sunni Arab guerrillas will keep hitting hard and the Sunni population "would certainly supply Iraqi guerrillas with the weapons needed to hound and harass U.S. troops"; Syria would raise hell; Iran would raise hell; the "international Salafi-Jihadi movement (what the U.S. tends to call al-Qaeda)" would raise hell; and to top it all "there is no safe place for an American base," be it near Baghdad or in Basra (southern Shi'ites might cut its lines of supply) or in Kurdistan (Turkey and Iraqi Kurds are virtually at war). Cole sums up the obvious: "A long-term U.S. base in Iraq is a crackpot neo-con fantasy."

The overwhelming majority of Sunni and Shi'ite Iraqis (but not the Kurds) want the end of the occupation—just like al-Zaidi. Before hurling his leather-soled missiles, al-Zaidi certainly had in mind Bush's true legacy in Iraq, which includes over a million dead and "disappeared" (directly or indirectly caused by the occupation), over 4 million internally and externally displaced, 70% unemployment, lack of electricity, lack of drinking water, a cholera epidemic, the balkanization of Baghdad—a shabby, dangerous collection of Sunni and Shi'ite ghettos separated by high blast walls—and the horrendously incompetent kleptocracy that calls itself the Iraqi Parliament.

The shoes also metaphorically hit the huge Bush administration army of advisers, analysts, sycophants, politicians, diplomats, generals, UN bureaucrats, businessmen, "human rights" wags, media hacks and assorted profiteers that made the Iraqi tragedy possible. And the shoes put to immense shame U.S. public opinion, who overwhelmingly condoned the

2003 invasion and occupation and only turned against it when facts on the ground and horrific non-stop carnage spelled out this was an "unwinnable" war.

Now contrast the shoes targeting Bush with Bush's last throes—his mandated "Operation Legacy" conducted by Texan Machiavelli Karl Rove (consisting of a 2-page list of talking points endlessly spun by outgoing Bush administration officials to gullible corporate media). Instead, a real-life "Operation Legacy" shortlist would include all the aspects of the Bush doctrine ("In what respect, Charlie?," as Sarah "Barracuda" Palin would say); the destruction of Afghanistan and Iraq and the possibility of destruction of Pakistan and Iran; the complete normalization of torture—and outsourcing of torture—as an "American value"; a monstrous national deficit that spells national bankruptcy; the destruction of the U.S. economy; and a repressive police state which spies on its citizens—ripping the U.S. Constitution and the Bill of Rights to shreds.

And there's more "legacy." The December 2008 Senate Armed Services Committee's report on the Bush administration's torture policy concluding, unanimously, and endorsed by all Republican senators, that it was the White House and not a bunch of bad apples that "damaged our ability to collect accurate intelligence that could save lives, strengthened the hand of our enemies, and compromised our moral authority." Or the unpublished 513-page federal history of the Iraq reconstruction, which the *New York Times* described as "a $100 billion failure caused by bureaucratic turf wars, spiraling violence and ignorance of the basic elements of Iraqi society and infrastructure."

Only a few days before al-Zaidi's act, in an interview published in the *Chicago Tribune* and the *Los Angeles Times*, President-elect Obama had promised, "We've got a unique opportunity to reboot America's image around the world and also in the Muslim world in particular... So we need to take advantage of that."

If Obama really wants to seize the "opportunity" and "reboot" America's image, he must convince the Muslim world that the U.S. will renounce, for good, the framework of the "war on terror" (or the

Pentagon's Long War) of which Obama is still prisoner; will renounce pre-emptive wars against Muslim countries; will stop demonizing them; will renounce the pathetic concept of "Islamo-fascism"; will practice an equitable foreign policy: and will not tolerate the slow-motion ethnic cleansing of Palestinians by the Israeli state. Supposing Obama would be able to deliver in all these issues, he could start with a speech in Baghdad. Not a Bush-style ultra-secretive appearance in a military base or in the Green Zone; but a speech in real-life, open air Baghdad, in Firdous Square for instance.

Or he could start with a speech in real-life, open air Kabul (and not, Bush-style, in Bagram airbase)—as Afghanistan is the heart of his new, proposed "surge." According to a December 2008 report by The International Council on Security and Development (ICOS), along with Kabul, another 72% of Afghanistan is now under a Taliban "permanent presence." Of four main roads leading into Kabul, the report diplomatically says three are "compromised" by the Taliban. No: they are in fact taken over by the Taliban.

Over 7 years after the fall of the Taliban and untold billions of dollars later, ICOS founder Norine MacDonald, in a shattering indictment of that elusive, comfy entity, the "international community," stated the obvious: "The majority of Afghans still lack access to basic necessities such as food and water... There is a danger that the Taliban will simply overrun Afghanistan under the noses of NATO"—which an overwhelming majority of Afghans, from Pashtuns to Tajiks, see as nothing else than Western occupiers. Once again: underdevelopment breeds "terror."

NATO's refrigerated noses anyway can barely protect their supply routes east to legendary Peshawar at the mouth of the Khyber pass—where NATO warehouses and shipping containers are routinely plundered by neo-Taliban. Not to mention that NATO-backed ISAF forces, UN bureaucrats and resident government missions barely see what's really happening on the ground in Afghanistan because they all live ensconced in mini-Green Zones. And on top of economic wasteland, no security and no development there's the gruesome U.S. and NATO-sponsored procession of Afghan civilians decimated by air strikes. There could not be a more graphic demonstration of the moral disgrace of the "war on terror"—the routinely macabre exercise of dropping $100,000 bombs on people making a dollar a day.

So the desperately impoverished civilian Afghan population is caught between absolute mistrust, bordering on hatred, of the "international community" and utter powerlessness facing wily Taliban coercion. McDonald spells out the obvious: "Until food, water and basic medicines are made available to the country's population, the people of Afghanistan will remain vulnerable to Taliban recruitment and Taliban propaganda against the West."

The signs are not good. By early December 2008 Gen. David McKiernan, the top U.S. commander in Afghanistan was asking the Pentagon for more than 20,000 soldiers, Marines and airmen.

He was adamant: U.S. troop levels of 55,000 to 60,000 in Afghanistan will be needed for "at least three or four more years. If we put these additional forces in here, it's going to be for the next few years. It's not a temporary increase of combat strength."

As Institute for Public Accuracy executive director Norman Solomon put it, "This fits the pattern of escalation of the Vietnam War. Rather than unveiling the plans for escalation all at once, the government releases information partially, in stages. The parable of the boiled frog comes to mind: the temperature is being raised one degree at a time, while Americans become gradually acclimated to an open-ended and escalating commitment to war in Afghanistan."

The U.S. needs a surge in Afghanistan: this is a cast-iron axiom at the top levels of the Obama presidency, on Capitol Hill and all over corporate media. Just as in the 2002 run up to the war on Iraq, dissenters are being silenced. Afghanistan may indeed be seen as a new Vietnam when we take into account a Pentagon mindset "continuity" spanning five decades. This is a faith-based issue: the Pentagon machine is capable of raising hell like no other, and that passes for "foreign policy."

Obama's National Security Advisor, General Jim Jones, oversaw the entire Guantanamo/Abu Ghraib period; supported the surge in Iraq; and has lobbied for extra humongous funds and extra 100,000 troops for the Pentagon—not to mention expanded militarization of the homeland. Blowback will be guaranteed—with Robert Gates once again in the cast of characters. As *Truthdig*'s Robert Scheer has pointed out, "this is the same Gates who in his 1996 memoir details how, as a member of the Carter administration, he was involved in supporting the *mujahideen* Islamic fighters against the secular government in Kabul six months before the Soviet invasion."

Before blowback comes to collect there will also be some "counterinsurgency" David Petraeus-in-Iraq-style to amuse the galleries. The Pentagon will buy local militias as part of the surrealistically denominated Afghanistan Social Outreach Program just as it bought the Sunni "Sons of Iraq" tribals. I've seen this game on the ground before, in eastern Afghanistan; warlords are already salivating with their potential profits. Pashtun "insurgents" will collect a few bucks while "working with NATO forces" and becoming "the first line of defense," as Pentagon jargon rules, then will merrily turn against them, as Afghan warriors have done for millennia.

One of the reasons the "Sons of Iraq" grew in numbers—apart from the $300 monthly salary in a land of 70% unemployment—was that tribal leaders in Anbar province wanted to get rid of al-Qaeda in the Land of the Two Rivers. There's absolutely nothing similar in Afghanistan—the "historic" al-Qaeda leadership is allegedly holed up in the Waziristans, in the impenetrable Pakistani tribal areas, and the multi-layered anti-occupation resistance in Afghanistan bears all shades of Talibanism that have nothing to do with al-Qaeda: as any student of Afghan warrior history knows, they want foreign occupiers out, period.

The Pentagon fears a Taliban/tribal Pashtun offensive to take over Kabul (the inevitable Taliban offensive happens every summer like clockwork); the new three to four combat brigades that will be sent by the summer of 2009 will mostly go to south of Kabul. Gates is on the record saying he will not have to downsize in Iraq to free up at least two of those three brigades for Afghanistan.

The elusive Mullah Omar, the leader of the historic Taliban who was last seen in the fall of 2001 running to obscure legend in the back of a Honda 50 cc and now is supposedly holed up in Quetta, Pakistan, with access to email, definitely is not trembling under his shawl. On Eid al-Adha, the Islamic festival of sacrifice, he fired a telling e-mail: "I would like to remind the illegal invaders who have invaded our defenseless and oppressed people that it is a golden opportunity for you at present to hammer out an exit strategy for your forces... The current armed clashes, which now number into tens, will spiral up to hundreds of armed clashes. Your current casualties of hundreds will jack up in to the thousands."

As Iran's Press TV reported slightly before Christmas 2008, Mullah Omar has presented an Afghan peace plan to Saudi King Abdullah. That includes: a timetable for NATO and U.S. withdrawal (the Obama presidency, under Pentagon pressure, would reject it); power-sharing with Karzai (Karzai himself would accept it); amnesty and incorporation of Taliban fighters into the Afghan army; and replacing NATO with peacekeeping forces from Muslim countries.

As much as the U.S., Iran would definitely not accept this plan. Especially because it involves a U.S.-approved mediation by an untrustworthy (from the point of view of Shi'ite Iran) Wahhabi partner— the House of Saud. Take the reaction of Parliament Speaker Ali Larijani, very close to Supreme Leader Ayatollah Khamenei and a strong candidate to win the Iranian presidency in the summer of 2009: "The trend is such that we should anticipate that the Taliban leader, Mullah Omar, will attend the White House's parties along with Western officials. If you could reach a compromise with terrorists so easily, why did you stage such a massacre in the region?"

As for the position of the true "deciders" in Washington, investigative historian Gareth Porter puts it in perspective: "If Obama were to express a willingness to negotiate a withdrawal timetable as part of a broader bargaining process, it would become the only effective form of leverage the

United States has on the Afghan government and on the Taliban. A rational government would gravitate quickly to that position in response to the realities in Afghanistan. I am certain that the Pentagon would ensure that no such option is considered."

1F. IRAN

It's fair to argue the Obama presidency won't be a *Blade Runner* replicant of the neo-cons in Iraq and will—eventually—leave for good. That has catapulted the neo-cons and Zio-cons' obsession to where it was in the first place: Iran (as in the 2003 motto "real men go to Tehran," not Baghdad).

Obama enters power just as the Iranian Islamic revolution enters its fourth decade, and a wide array of Obama's foreign policy team—from UN Ambassador Susan Rice and Secretary of State Hilary Clinton to Richard Holbrooke, Tom Daschle and Dennis Ross are humanitarian neo-cons very close to think tank/armchair hawk lairs such as the Washington Institute for Near East Policy (WINEP) or the American Enterprise Institute (AEI).

Frantic spinning even before Obama's inauguration produced stuff like the Israeli *Ha'aretz* daily attributing to Obama, via an unnamed source, the guarantee for Israel of an "atomic umbrella" to face the threat of an Iranian nuclear attack.

For this armchair warrior crowd, the ideal *modus operandi* towards "victory" remains the same: "tough" diplomacy; diplomacy breaks down; other options on the table; naval blockade; provocation; Iranian response; U.S. attack.

In a series of eye-opening reports for Inter Press Service from Tehran in December 2008, investigative historian Gareth Porter carefully described the dynamics of the internal debate in Iran. One strand sees Obama as "an opportunity for Iran to find a way out of its decades-long conflict with the United States," the other views Obama as "subject to the control of powerful forces -- especially the pro-Israel lobby."

The Ultimate Decider is of course the Supreme Leader, Ayatollah Ali Khamenei, who himself spent months prodding advisers and state officials to forge a consensus. And it's the Supreme Leader that Obama must address.

Mahan Abedin, director of research of the London-based Center for the Study of Terrorism has pointed out the Great Wall (or "wall of mistrust," as it is known in Tehran) between the U.S. and the Islamic Republic's clerical leadership, who he correctly describes as "the most serious and effective anti-American force in the world."

In an interview with the Fars News Agency, which is very close to the Islamic Revolutionary Guards Corps (IRGC), banned in the U.S. as a "terrorist organization" Ebrahim Asgharzadeh, a top student leader during the occupation of the American Embassy (or "Den of Espionage" as its is known in Tehran) on November 1979, and a top revolution ideologue, stressed the Iranian Revolution poses a permanent and fundamental contradiction to American interests. Talk about an understatement.

"Anti-Americanism" is always a reductionist slogan: in Iran it is a very complex phenomenon, and taken extremely seriously. It's all about the nefarious consequences of U.S. foreign policy—and spans everyone beyond the clerical establishment, from the secular extreme left and the Islamic left (which includes former President Mohammad "dialogue of civilizations" Khatami and his wide-ranging reformist supporters) to ultra-nationalists and monarchists. It always comes back to the root of it all—the CIA-coordinated coup against the nationalist/ democratic government of Prime Minister Mohammad Mossadegh (we will touch upon that in part 2).

This mindset also happens to merge with a dominant narrative among the European left. Take for instance political philosophy master Antonio "Empire" Negri, who is fascinated by the two-pronged "political production" of Iran, which leads to "the country's independence on an international level" and also to "a strong autonomization of the society in relation to the state." In *Goodbye Mr. Socialism* Negri more or less sums up the Iranian national mood: "We are in favor of a real and secular democracy, but if the Israelis attacked our country, we would side with the imams."

Washington neo-cons, of course—not to mention the rightwing noise machine—had never even bothered to understand this contradiction. Negri sees it as an expression of profound independence, radical freedom and an "acceptance to delegate political power to the Shi'ite hierarchy." Well, it's slightly more complicated than that.

As far as Iranians' "incredible freedom across the lower middle classes," in spite of the clerics' religious monopoly, Negri may be partially right (during the Ahmadinejad years the moral police went on overdrive and curtailed this "incredible freedom.") As for popular "acceptance," that's even more complicated, because the clerics are widely ridiculed as corrupt and incompetent by the urbanized middle class (that was one of the reasons of Ahmadinejad's initial popular appeal; he was a "man of the people," not a cleric).

Negri applauds how the oil and gas income, "controlled by the Shi'ite hierarchy, is transferred through assistance missions to the Iranian proletariat." Well, not that smoothly: Ahmadinejad and his ideological team have amply demonstrated that they are as ignorant of economics as Shi'ite clerics. When Negri says that "the people accepts, more or less, this situation" and may "count on a working welfare state" similar to Venezuela's, with good schools, hospitals and aid to families, it's also not that rosy. It all boils down to the government's incompetent economic management.

Iranians essentially get by because as an eschatological—and revolutionary—religion, fueled by a mix of romanticism and despair, Shi'ism has always been deeply intertwined with poverty and communal solidarity. But Negri is right when he stresses the merits of the wealth redistribution system in the Islamic republic, comparing Khomeinism with projects for socialist modernization. Now try selling this idea in the U.S. red states.

Ideologically and strategically, Obama in power slightly changes the equation only in terms of a tactical thaw between two formidable and virtually irreconcilable foes – the "imperial" U.S. ruling elite faction and the Khomeinists.

The question for Obama is: how to approach Ayatollah Khamenei? Which interlocutor to choose to bridge the gap? A very good pick would be wily pragmatist and former president Akbar Hashemi Rafsanjani, who for that matter has very solid contacts in Washington. Another good pick would be Khatami—even though he's too progressive for Khamenei. Ahmadinejad—as Russian intelligentsia has been betting for months—may be on the way out in the summer of 2009 elections. The new President may be former nuclear negotiator and current Parliament speaker Ali Larijani, a Supreme Leader golden boy.

Ayatollah Khamenei may have the charisma of a bowl of lentils, but he's a complex character. He's of course *primus inter pares* among the clerical elite. But he's even closer to the Hezbollahi grassroots—the salt of the revolutionary earth (the regime grassroots is in the tens of millions). He has always supported Ahmadinejad, but then almost lost his patience when Ahmadinejad caused endless diplomatic problems to the regime because of his incendiary rhetoric.

A true measure of Khamenei's power was provided by that supreme chess board—the December 2006 election for the Council of Experts, won by Rafsanjani's moderate faction. This electrifying election essentially pitted two factions at the very top the regime—the moderate/pragmatists (led by Rasfanjani) and the extreme right (led by Ayatollah Mesbah Yazdi, the *eminence grise* and spiritual leader of Ahmadinejad.) As the lively press in Tehran gleefully dubbed it, it was the battle between the reclusive "crocodile" Yazdi against the eternal insider, relative 'friend of the West', former President, lifelong opportunist and king of the dodgy deal, the "shark" Rafsanjani.

The "shark" and his faction won, hands down. The Council of Experts (86 clerics only; no women allowed) is key because it's the only institution in the Islamic Republic capable of holding the Supreme Leader to account and even removing him from office. It is the system's Holy Grail.

There had been rumors in Tehran all through 2006 that "the crocodile" and his followers were making a naked power grab. They had won city and village council elections, then parliamentary elections and the presidency (with Ahmadinejad), and were ready to conquer the Council of Experts and thus be in a position to choose the next Supreme Leader.

Ayatollah Yazdi and his followers have always stressed they want to implement "real Islam." They view the Rafsanjani camp as a bunch of filthy rich, morally and legally corrupt decadents, totally oblivious to the concerns of 'ordinary people', whose self-styled key symbol happens to be Ahmadinejad. Yazdi is also the spiritual mentor of the Hojjatieh, a sort of ultra-fundamentalist sect whose literal interpretation of Shi'ite tradition holds that chaos in mankind is a necessary precondition for the imminent arrival of the Mahdi (the twelfth "hidden Imam"). Ahmadinejad himself may not be a Hojjatieh, but he totally understands where they're coming from.

Even going downhill, and perhaps losing the presidency, the Ahmadinejad/Yazdi faction will still maintain a huge, countrywide popular base in the military-security establishment, in the tens of millions, ranging from the Revolutionary Guard Pasdaran to the Bassijis, the hardcore paramilitary militia, also known in Iran as "the army of 20 million," and expanding to the pious, apolitical, downtrodden masses, mostly rural but also urban (in sprawling south Tehran, for instance).

The only crucial policy the Council of Experts has implemented since the beginning of the Islamic Revolution has been to appoint Khamenei as Khomeini's successor and new Supreme Leader, in 1989. It was in fact a white coup—because according to the constitution at the time the Supreme Leader had to be a *marja* (source of imitation and top religious leader). Khamenei was definitely not up to it. Khomeini died while the constitution was being revised; so Khamenei was in fact appointed by a law ratified only after he was already installed as Supreme Leader.

Yazdi tried a different strategy: to take over the Council of Experts from the inside and then overwhelm Khamenei. The Supreme Leader played a very deft hand. He firmly supported Yazdi before the 2005 presidential election, but then discreetly rallied his followers—and the full machinery of the system—to keep Yazdi and his protégé Ahmadinejad under control. Over the years Khamenei has been politicizing the religious system non-stop, to the point of the Islamic Republic nowadays being neither a democracy nor a theocracy: rather, it's a clerical autocracy.

For all his outrageous non-diplomatic outbursts Ahmadinejad, after all, broke new grounds—at least in the framework of the Islamic Republic. He openly offered face-to-face talks and normalization of U.S.-Iran relations—and was not stoned to death for it by the core revolutionary hardliners. He's been to New York four times—to address the UN General Assembly. There is a possibility of the National Iranian American Council opening an office in Tehran (hardliners complained it would be a Trojan Horse).

The neo-cons—wallowing in their disinformation mire and ideological turpitude—never understood that a U.S. attack would never be able to provoke "regime change" in Iran. The clerics know it. The Iranian population knows it. Serious Iran observers like Trita Parsi know it. The question for Obama—assuming his commitment to talking with no preconditions—is how to dissuade the "clerical autocracy" leaders from their hyperbolic, 30-year-long obsession in projecting Iran as the only authentic and serious counter power to American hyperpower in the world. It's easy to imagine the Cuban revolutionaries' pride in standing up to relentless imperial pressure since the early 1960s. Now turbo-charge this feeling applied to the heirs of one of the most ancient and sophisticated civilizations the world has ever known.

At least pragmatists on the U.S. side are getting the message. By December 2008, at a forum in the Brookings Institution marking 30 years since the establishment of formal U.S. relations with China, former U.S. national security adviser to Jimmy Carter and campaign adviser to Obama, Zbigniew Brzezinski urged Washington to establish ties with Iran: "One of the reasons that I do favor a dialogue with the Iranians, and if it is feasible, the establishment of normal diplomatic relationships, is that I think that would help promote political change in a country which is far less centrally controlled, far less subject to effective state authority than was or is the case in the People's Republic of China." And this after Brzezinski had told *Ha'aretz* that "[The military option] is not a real option for the U.S. and it is not a real option for Israel because Israel doesn't have a capability to destroy Iranian nuclear facilities."

Well, although employing some tortuous reasoning—there's very effective state authority in Iran; and the U.S./Israel military option is renounced only because it's impractical—at least Dr. Brzezinski has got this one right.

1G. LATIN AMERICA

Even before its Lincolnesque inauguration the Obama presidency and Latin America already seemed to be on a collision course.

On December 16, 2008, in a groundbreaking, wide-ranging, 33-country Latin American and Caribbean summit coordinated by the Brazilian government, Raúl Castro—in his first trip abroad since taking over from Fidel in 2006—saw Cuba accepted as the 23rd member of the Group of Rio political forum, a body created in 1986 to promote Latin American cooperation. All the leaders at the summit ecstatically proclaimed: "This is a historic moment." Then the forum immediately condemned and demanded the end of the U.S. embargo against Cuba in effect since February 1962.

So it's not an accident that on the same day Bush's Secretary of Commerce Carlos Gutierrez, a fierce anti-Castro Cuban-American, declared the U.S. will not lift the embargo. The leaders gathered at the summit took it for what it was: not only a "message" to Latin America but a torpedo launched towards the Obama submarine. One thing is certain, though: "The wall has been pierced," as Argentinian daily *Página 12* headlined. The U.S. strategy towards Latin America has completely failed—and Obama will have to pick up the pieces.

Even before the Obama inauguration, Michael Shifter, vice-president of the Inter-American Dialogue in Washington, stressed "the issues that have dominated Latin America relations—immigration, U.S. trade barriers on agricultural products, and Cuba—remained in dispute." Shifter said, "Latin America wants the U.S. to be engaged, but in very different terms that it has in the past. In any case, they're not owaiting around for the U.S. to change its mindset."

The *New York Times* was reduced to carping about the U.S. being "dismissed" from the summit in Brazil. No wonder: for anyone who had not already noticed it, the summit buried for good the 1823 Monroe doctrine, which declared Latin America off-limits to European powers.

Not only the U.S. was not invited—the same happened to former colonial powers Spain and Portugal as well. Brazilian Foreign Minister Celso Amorim praised "countries of all ideological strands harboring the common desire of integrating Latin American and the Caribbean as their common space." Amorim does not see hegemony as a good deal even for the U.S. itself: "They don't want it, and it's not feasible. This doesn't mean we can't have a very good relation with the U.S."

The only absent heads of state happened to be two close Bush administration pals, Peru's Alan Garcia and Colombia's Alvaro Uribe.

As for Raúl Castro, he was the true star of the show. Very diplomatic, he did not attack the U.S. frontally, but roundly condemned neoliberal policies and attributed the global financial crisis to an "unjust and selfish economic order."

Castro is nonetheless hopeful: "If Mr. Obama wants to have a discussion, we will. It's increasingly difficult to isolate Cuba. We are small, but we have shown we cannot be easily dominated." He denied that Brazilian President Lula offered to be a mediator between himself and Obama.

For his part Lula did send a clear message to Obama, saying his U.S. presidential victory would truly become historic only when he lifts the U.S. blockade on Cuba: "This has no economic explanation, no political explanation, it is meaningless." Lula definitely has his eyes set on the big picture. The Foreign Ministry considers Brazil to be one of the very few countries in the world capable of establishing a simultaneous dialogue with Cuba, Venezuela's Chávez and an Obama administration.

Raúl Castro, compared with legendary "Comandante" Fidel, is more of a moderate, politically and economically. After a groundbreaking visit to an ailing Fidel by Lula in early 2008, Raúl started to consider the possibility of Cuba distancing itself a teeny bit from Venezuela without of course hurting Chávez's feelings. Lula's Workers Party's close ties with Cuba and Fidel have been very solid since the 1970s. What the Brazilian Foreign Ministry has suggested is for Raúl to make a gesture towards the international community—if not a gradual but significant political opening, at least the release of political prisoners. This would prove Cuba has embarked on a genuine transition and is not simply reproducing the Chinese model in Latin America.

At the summit, Lula was his optimistic best: "There was a time when brother Hugo Chávez was alone. Who could have imagined, ten years ago, that our dear Evo Morales would be the President of Bolivia? Who could have imagined that a liberation theology bishop [Fernando Lugo] would be President of Paraguay?" Evo—stressing Latin American solidarity with Havana, and successive, anti-embargo UN resolutions—proposed Latin America delivers an official deadline for the U.S. to suspend the economic blockade.

Chávez for his part stressed the global financial crisis "has the effect of a thousand hurricanes," and that requires Latin American and Caribbean regional integration, while Paraguay's Fernando Lugo blamed "structural asymmetries." Chávez, in his trademark Garcia Márquez literary character ranting mode, insisted the crisis will get worse because capitalism is not "Obama's or Bush's, it is evil." He sees the capitalist world "tumbling down" as a consequence of the global crisis, and the cause is the Washington model imposed on the rest of the world; Chávez praises instead Lula's "Latin-Americanist" thinking.

A case can be made that Brazil and Venezuela are fiercely positioning themselves for regional leadership. Brazil is a natural leader of Mercosur (the South American common market) and Unasur (the Union of South American nations) while Venezuela is a natural leader of ALBA (the Bolivarian Alternative for the Americas). ALBA was launched in 2005 by

Venezuela as a counterpunch to the Bush administration's failed offensive of the Free Trade Area of the Americas (FTAA). Unasur was formed in May 2008 by 12 countries to mediate serious conflicts such as the separatists vs. government clashes in Bolivia, thus bypassing the discredited, U.S.-dominated Organization of American States (OAS).

But it's all interlinked; Mercosur, for instance, will absorb Bolivian exports boycotted by the U.S. as "punishment" for Bolivia expelling the DEA, whose agents were accused of conspiring to overthrow Evo. Chávez seems to be comfortable with the interlocking mechanisms—he prefers to identify an emerging collective regional leadership, "leader countries, male leaders, female leaders, people's leaders."

The CIA, feeling threatened, or out of sheer ignorance, depreciatively dismisses Latin America's center-left concerted push towards autonomy instead of dependence as a push towards a "Caliphate" (in relation to the imperial center; China and India are also considered "Caliphates"). All bets are off on how the Obama presidency will adapt to the new Latin American "political-ideological profile," as Lula put it, and that includes, of course, expanded diplomatic, economic and military ties with China, Russia and Iran.

That means Russian warships—including a nuclear cruiser—in joint naval exercises with Venezuela, a first since the Cold War; a Russian destroyer visiting Havana's harbor amid great fanfare; Chinese President Hu Jintao signing a free-trade agreement with Peru; Lula inviting Iranian President Mahmoud Ahmadinejad for a state visit; and Ecuador's President Rafael Correa refusing to renew the lease on the U.S.'s Manta base, defended by the Bush administration as a critical platform for the "war on drugs"—an assumption widely ridiculed all over South America.

Chávez has bought $4.4 billion in weapons from Russia after the Bush administration blocked sales of aircraft parts to Venezuela. Brazil and France signed a deal for four nuclear submarines to patrol Brazil's rich Atlantic oil basins. China, and not the U.S., is now Chile's biggest copper export market; in fact a New Copper Road, sea lane rather, is on from the South Pacific to East Asia.

China is Cuba's second largest trading partner (after Venezuela), with annual bilateral trade at over $2.6 billion. **China has pledged $10 billion in loans to Brazil's oil giant Petrobras to develop the Western Hemisphere's largest oil discovery since 1976.** And by 2012 Caracas will be selling one million barrels of oil a day to Beijing. No wonder Chinese President Hu Jintao declared at the 2008 APEC summit in Peru that "China and South America have already become extremely good friends and partners."

Julia Sweig, director of the Latin America program at the Council of Foreign Relations, sums it all up: "Monroe certainly would be rolling over in his grave."

The Bush administration's countermove—resurrecting the Fourth Fleet from the dead after 58 years to ostensibly "patrol the Caribbean"—sent shivers all over Latin America. Chávez threatened to sink them. Lula demanded an official explanation from the Bush administration.

Chávez-demonization anyway remains a burgeoning cottage industry in Washington. As the groundbreaking summit in Brazil went on, over 100 top experts on Latin America were sending an open letter to the Board of Directors of Human Rights Watch blasting a recent report on Venezuela, *A Decade Under Chávez: Political Intolerance and Lost Opportunities for Advancing Human Rights in Venezuela*, stressing that it "does not meet even the most minimal standards of scholarship, impartiality, accuracy, or credibility." The signers included leading scholars from Harvard, Johns Hopkins and NYU and from Argentina, Australia, Brazil, Mexico, the U.K. and Venezuela.

Obama's foreign policy attention will be totally focused on the Pentagon-coined "arc of instability" from the Middle East to Central Asia. But all over Latin America he's the subject of enormous expectations. During the campaign, Obama opposed an FTA with Colombia, on the—correct—grounds of vicious state repression of workers and peasants. Obama will have to confront Alvaro Uribe and determine any meaningful change to Plan Colombia—a Pentagon "war on terror" gambit disguised as a failed, Clinton-born anti-drug program. He has promised to increase U.S. economic aid to Latin America; governments don't want aid, they want partnerships. He also pledged to meet with Chávez and Raúl Castro "without preconditions" (and then backtracked). He claimed he is "committed" to Latin America. But how will he interpret the new rules of the game—a fast integrating Latin America where the U.S. is just another player among many?

1H. RUSSIA/NATO

How Obama—and the Pentagon—will, if at all, modify the agenda of encircling Russia with NATO? In late 2008 NATO ministers in Brussels read the writing on the wall and decided to in fact indefinitely delay the admission of Georgia and the Ukraine. NATO in fact promised Russia not to expand eastward in exchange for a new military deal. New NATO members like Poland and the Baltic countries were resolutely stomped down by "old Europe."

Those progressives who dream of Obama advocating NATO to be dissolved must have smoked some prime Jamaican. A common theme in the salons of Paris and London is that cowardly European leaders will always indulge in believing they are part of the same Washington elite of global deciders. Analysts less drenched with Margaux would argue that Europe has no independent foreign policy because what it really wants has always been forbidden by the U.S., and has no independent security policy because it continued to participate in NATO, which is controlled by the U.S. NATO as an armed wing of continental expansionism is a social and political dead end. But the game—which involves Pipelineistan, as we'll see in part 2—is far from over. As F. William Engdahl has pointed out, writing on Global Research, "the strategy of bringing Georgia and Ukraine into NATO is part of a far larger and more dangerous strategic long-term plan of Washington to ultimately encircle, confront and dismember Russia as a functioning state."

As much as Secretary of State Hillary Clinton and Pentagon supremo Robert Gates will continue lobbying for two *causes celebres*—NATO expansion and the Reagan-era "Star Wars" missile defense system—French President Nikolas Sarkozy will favor Russian President Dmitry Medvedev's proposal for "a new security architecture" which will counter both. It's just like the return of the living dead—in this case Rumsfeld's "unknown unknowns" of "old Europe" vs. "new Europe" plus, once again, the Clinton 1990s: after all it was Bill Clinton who in 1994 heavily started advancing NATO expansion. Unlike the Eastern European nebula, the French and the Germans wisely understand where Russia is coming from.

It doesn't help the Obama presidency the fact that Hilary Clinton has been a sucker for a Bush-style "American pre-eminence"/"**America's standing in the world**" ideological, unipolar mindset. Hillary Clinton, on her own instincts, will never treat Russia as an equal. Konstantin Kosachyov, head of the Foreign Relations Committee of Russia's lower house of Parliament, has been on the record saying "these [Obama's] nominations inspire no optimism whatsoever."

Russia—as well as the Shanghai Cooperation Organization (SCO), not to mention Western Europe and Latin America—are all about a multipolar new world order. In his famous 2007 speech at the Munich Conference on Security Policy, then President Vladimir Putin blasted Clinton-style "ideological stereotypes, double standards and other typical aspects of Cold War bloc thinking."

As for Gates, from his early days at the CIA he has been a Star Wars junkie. In 1986 Gates gave a speech called *The Soviets and SDI—Strategic Defense Initiative* in which he argued that because of Soviet Union technological breakthroughs the U.S. had to invest rivers of dollars just to catch up. Gates even "predicted" the Soviet Union would launch their own missile defense system by the late 1980s. Lately he has been frantically lobbying European governments in favor of a missile defense system for protection against "rogue states"—code for Iran. The Pentagon now has 21 missile interceptors in Alaska and California. The Bush administration wants 10 missile interceptors in Poland and a missile tracking radar in the Czech Republic by 2014. As of November 2008, Gates' official position is that "Russia has nothing to fear from a defensive missile shield."

The strategic benefit may be dubious enough; but what about the technological imperatives? No one really knows whether the system—which has already burned $110 billion in federal money—works at all. The

Pentagon invariably spins "successful tests." In pure spy vs. spy cartoon fashion, some of the tests were rigged—like the Pentagon putting a GPS on the target missiles so they can be easily intercepted. A common Washington joke is that for neo-cons "missile defense is a theology, not a technology." The Holy Grail of neo-con theology in this case is being able to nuke without fear of being nuked back. Then, all is set for the advent of the New American Century.

Obama promised in the campaign trail early on to "end misguided defense policies" and "cut investments in unproven missile defense systems." Then he backtracked. In the first presidential debate with McCain, he said "I actually believe that we need missile defense because of Iran and North Korea and the potential for them to obtain or to launch nuclear weapons."

Immediately after Obama's election Medvedev took no time to spell it out; missile defense in Poland means Russian missiles near the Polish border: "We might reverse this decision if the new U.S. administration is going to once again review and analyze all the consequences of its decisions to deploy missiles and radars."

It will get worse, much worse. In mid-December 2008 General Nikolai Makarov, chief of the General Staff of Russia's Armed Forces told the *RIA Novosti* agency "the U.S. has opened bases in Romania and Bulgaria, and according to our information plans to establish them in Kazakhstan and Uzbekistan." That's NATO's encirclement of Russia meets the war on terror surge in Afghanistan. The U.S. already has a base at Manas airport near Bishkek, in Kyrgyzstan.

As much as Obama will be focused on Iraq/Afghanistan, the real drama will be how not to provoke Russia as the U.S. addresses a divided Europe that is not even exactly sure what NATO is up to.

11. CHINA

U.S. foreign policy circles have been deluged with the same old scratchy CD talk of "bringing China into the fold," make "China play by the rules," "integration as the new containment," China's "readiness to become a good citizen" and other U.S.-centric platitudes. Let's try something completely different.

In mid-September 2008 a group of scholars all across China gathered in a massive Stalinist hall surrounded by a sea of gleaming glitzy towers in Shanghai at the third annual World Forum on China Studies to ostensibly discuss China's new role in a (multipolar) world. Soon the consensus set in: they were in fact debating the merits of a superior civilization in the post-American world.

Zheng Bijian, former vice-chair of the Central Party School, very close to the Communist Party leadership and no less than the author of China's "peaceful rise" doctrine, argued that China's dream of dodging Western domination since the Opium War (1840-42) was finally attained in the "new awakening" following the Little Helmsman Deng Xiaoping's reforms, which were started over three decades ago, in December 1978. Now fully awakened, China had embarked on "a hundred schools of thought" (echoes of Mao) on how to profit from the globalized economy.

What a long, fabulous trip it's been—from working for the big commune, living in crappy houses with oil lamps and no toilets, eating a maximum of 400 g of maize flour and potatoes a day, and having to daily carry water from the well, to living in the "factory of the world," the world's fourth largest economy growing on average by 9.8% a year for three decades non-stop.

The historic turning point was of course the third plenum of the 11th Central Committee of the Chinese Communist Party, when Deng, after finally sidelining the Maoist gang, launched his economic reforms—a process he cautiously defined as "crossing the river by feeling the stones."

Success achieved, the challenge now is how to deal with the global economic crisis—when Chinese GDP growth may fall from a staggering 11.9% in 2007 to 5% in 2009, with industrial production and exports falling sharply. President Hu Jintao has described the outlook as extremely worrying. There will be blood—peasant protests, mingguo (itinerant workers) protests, even middle class protests. Inequality—although not as stark as in the U.S.—is a key factor. A December 2008 report from the

Chinese Academy of Social Sciences showed the average income of the richest 20% of Chinese households is now 17 times as high as that of the poorest 20%. It's a multi-layered fissure between rich and poor, the coast and the hinterland, the city and the village.

For all the excitement at the Shanghai summit, the Chinese model is far from perfect. There's endemic corruption; and price controls or lack of competition in many sectors lead to overlapping distortions. It's an export-dependent model; the domestic market has got to expand—the key target of a late 2008 $586 billion New Deal package.

"In the short term, expanding infrastructure investment is a key issue for stimulating domestic demand; but in the longer term, improving public services development is more important," according to Wang Xiaolu, deputy director of China's National Economic Research Institute. "If our citizens worry about their children's education fees or healthcare in the future or housing issues, they will tend to save money instead of spending. Only when the public services are well developed will citizens dare to spend the money they earn."

China is used to facing unbeatable odds. Never joke with an ancient civilization. At the Shanghai summit, Zheng compared the current historical juncture, at least before the global economic crisis, to the Spring and Autumn Period (770-476 B.C.) and the Warring States Period (475-221 B.C.). It was hard to refute Zheng's demonstration: an "awakened" China had proved its superiority over the lofty Western theories of "a clash of civilizations" and the triumph of the West at "the end of history" by solving the "riddle of the century": how to lift hundreds of millions of Chinese out of poverty and underdevelopment by applying Deng's "to get rich is glorious" stratagems.

So neo-Confucian Deng Xiaoping was wise to "seek truth from facts" and, step by step, like feeling his way across a shallow river, "construct socialism" with Chinese characteristics. So this was the real Third Way, not Tony Blair's: a model to the developing world beyond the Western models of conflict or domination.

Don't mess with the new China—which for all the challenges ahead would never choose the Western way, "with their colonialist plundering of the world's resources in the process of industrialization" and would not seek superpower status like the former Soviet Union "under the cover of the so-called world revolution." The new China is all about an "open, non-exclusive and harmonious" relationship with the rest of the world.

Also during the summit, Zhang Xianglong, professor of Philosophy at Beijing University stressed the "non-universalist" nature of Confucianism—and truth being found in particular, concrete circumstances instead of universally applicable standards. Talk about Chinese pragmatism! Instantly dismissed were the Western concept of universal human rights and democracy and the Marxist concept of universal laws of development. Because it is non-universal, Confucian or neo-Confucian civilization goes for "pragmatic discourse." And Deng was nothing else than the Great Pragmatist. As a framework for establishing a true East-West dialogue, Obama the Pragmatist could not hope for anything more auspicious.

Zheng claimed that China had found a harmonious Third Way. For his part Zhang argued that a "clash of civilizations" or the "end of history" can "only occur when universalist cultures encounter each other or prevail over each other. When two non-universalist cultures meet, there may well be friction; but total warfare that aims at mutual annihilation is generally avoided. When, however, two universalist cultures meet, even though they may compromise and negotiate to ensure their temporary safety, in the long run they are in principle engaged in a to-the-death struggle."

That's how Buddhism and Taoism coexisted for millennia in China and how Confucian virtue is the basis of China's soft power. But China has gone beyond it all. For Tan Chung, former dean of the Centre for East Asian Studies at Nehru University, what we are witnessing is the transition of the world from a "geopolitical paradigm" to the "geo-civilizational paradigm" in which China, of course, is paramount. "Awakened" China is thus all about integration of civilizations through harmonious co-existence. Tan mentioned as an example the 5,000 years of harmonious coexistence between India and China -- only interrupted by the 20 years between 1958 and 1978 when both civilizations were "infected" with Western nationalist notions; the Central Asian fusion of Serindia; and the Southeast Asia fusion of Indochina.

On the other hand, in the West, "all the brilliant ancient civilizations like Babylonia, Egypt, Greece and Rome have become ruins without being handed down. This was because there was no 'geo-civilizational paradigm' among them. The 'geopolitical paradigm' pushed them to scramble for territory and indulge in mutual destruction. The basic difference between Eastern and Western hemispheres lies here."

So China has awakened from the "nightmare of history" (copyright James Joyce) and is back to its "civilizational vocation": harmonious culture. Tan illustrated it by quoting the famous Confucius adage in the *Analects*: the state of Qi—which pursues power—is to turn into the state of Lu—which seeks higher cultural development -- and ultimately merger into the Tao, or truth-prevailing state.

Politically, is neo-Confucian China capable of influencing the West? Zhang Wei-Wei, one of Deng Xiaoping's favorite interpreters, predicts that as world power is shifting towards Asia, the Western-promoted "democracy vs. autocracy" debate that gets the Beijing leadership so incensed will be replaced by a pragmatic "good governance vs. bad governance" debate. The Chinese are confident the Confucian notion of authority will prevail: but it's hard to see the West re-evaluating Deng's decision to crush China's "rebellious children" in Tiananmen in 1989 as wise—and all in the name of "internal harmony."

A case can be made that—for all the excitement over Obama's historic election—ever since Eisenhower's prescient but sadly ineffectual warning in 1960, the American President is limited to running a very powerful, Corporatistan/ "military-industrial complex," and not to change it. Especially in times of dire economic crisis—when the ruling classes circle the wagons and the working masses pay for it.

Backtracking in history, a case can also be made than when China was at its peak—and that has been most of the time in these past two millennia—the Chinese ruling class did not see the Europeans coming and remaking the world through creative destruction, turning Eurasia inside out. Europe had blasted a new frontier—the sea—while China's mindset was still mired in the steppes.

Now "son of Europe" U.S. is in decline and China—after a "short" spell, as any Chinese would tell us—is back. Obama has already lived in Asia—in multicultural Indonesia. But he will have a long journey before inspiring trust not only in China but all across Asia. So to reach his Holy Grail, Obama the Pragmatist may have to heed the call—if not physically at least spiritually: Go East, young man.

2: OBAMA PLAYS PIPELINEISTAN

As his discreet and once vastly influential geopolitical mentor/adviser Zbig Brzezinski may have already rhapsodized to him in graphic detail, President Obama has been hurled right into the volcano—the battlefield for the control of Eurasia, also known as the new New Great Game, the crucial plot in the ongoing rush towards a new, non-U.S.-centric world order.

In his 1997 opus *The Grand Chessboard*, Realpolitik Zbig—a consultant for BP during the Clinton administration who went to Baku to sell the BTC pipeline idea—enunciated in detail how to keep U.S. "global primacy." Later, his master plan was duly incorporated by that bunch of wacky but dangerous Dr. Nos congregated at Bill Kristol's Neo-con Central, the infamous Project for a New American Century (PNAC), whose website recently returned from the dead.

Dr. Zbig himself, somewhat reluctantly, returned to the spotlight during the 2008 U.S. presidential campaign, even sharing a book of interviews with General Brent Scowcroft. For these two A-list, slick informed strategists, whom Steve Clemons from the *Washington Note* blog calls the "Walter Matthau and Jack Lemmon of U.S. foreign policy" everything ultimately harks back to page 198 of *The Grand Chessboard*: "... to prevent the emergence of a hostile coalition that could eventually seek to challenge America's primacy, not to mention the remote possibility of any one particular state seeking to do so."

As for the emergence of "strategically compatible partners" along the way, that's fine as long as they are "prompted by American leadership" to shape "a more cooperative trans-Eurasian security system."

Dr. Zbig's clincher comes on page 215: "The U.S. policy goal must be unapologetically twofold: to perpetuate America's own dominant position for at least a generation and preferably longer still." That won't happen. And then there's "a prolonged phase of gradually expanding cooperation with key Eurasian partners, both stimulated and arbitrated by America."

Implicit is that imperial America rules, and satrapies follow. That also won't happen.

In a further twist around the everlasting saga of those who control power also controlling weapons, money and the Word, the "war on terror," which the Pentagon slyly rebranded The Long War, sports a doppelganger: a global energy war. In *Globalistan*, with a hat tip to sociologist Zygmunt Bauman, I called it Liquid War. This war, of course—but not exclusively—flows via pipelines,.

In a few vignettes I will try to sketch at least some of the moves in the maddeningly complex chessboard of the new New Great Game. Forget about al-Qaeda and Taliban and the "war on terror" galvanizing all the media attention. These are minor diversions. The ultra high-stakes, hardcore geopolitical game—Liquid War—flows along *these* lines. Who said Pipelineistan couldn't be fun?

2A. THE CHINESE ENIGMA

The world's known, proven gas reserves so far may last only 70 years, and oil reserves only 40 years. Even considering the current global recession, world demand for natural gas will triple up to 2020.

In the summer of 2008 oil reached $147 a barrel. By the end of 2008 it had plunged to below $50 a barrel. Merrill Lynch was projecting a drop to $25 in 2009. The most optimistic forecasts—incorporating a huge OPEC production cut decided in December 2008—barely reach a temporary $60 a barrel. That should spell major trouble to producer countries. Russia's 2009 budget was designed for oil at $95 a barrel; Venezuela's for $60; and Iran's for also $60. Brazil's Petrobras, on the other hand, wisely projected $35 a barrel.

Whatever the short-term scenario it's still oil that will be a key engine in the inexorable transfer of economic power from the West to Asia. By 2025, Asia will be importing 80% of its oil. And 80% of this total will be from the Persian Gulf.

In *Rising Powers, Shrinking Planet: The New Geopolitics of Energy* Michael Klare has identified the key vectors of this new world order—

ranging from scarcity of primary energy supplies to "the painfully slow development of energy alternatives" (based on current rates of development and investment, the U.S. Department of Energy projects that in 2030, fossil fuels will still account for exactly the same share of world energy as in 2004—less than 8%).

A wild global scramble, law-of-the-jungle-style—i.e. Liquid War—will be paramount. By 2010, the developing world will be consuming no less than 40% of the world's energy. China alone will gobble up 17% by 2015, and 20% by 2025. Thus the multi-layered Chinese strategy for competing with the Western "majors," from Sinopec's strategic alliance with Saudi Aramco to China National Petroleum Corporation (CNPC) alliances with Russia's Gazprom and Venezuela's PDVSA (a matter of getting that precious extra-heavy crude from the Orinoco belt which was once in Chevron's bag).

There will be an inexorable "migration of power and wealth from energy-deficit to energy-surplus nations." Klare stresses how in the case of oil and natural gas, 10 oil-rich states possess 82.2% of the world's proven reserves (from top to bottom: Saudi Arabia, Iran, Iraq, Kuwait, the United Arab Emirates, Venezuela, Russia, Libya, Kazakhstan, and Nigeria); and 3 gas-rich states -- Russia, Iran, and Qatar—hold 55.8% of the world supply. Klare did not even include the most recent fabulous estimates for Turkmenistan, the gas republic. Anyway, the corollary remains an astonishing transfer of wealth from West to East—illustrated, for instance, by oil states' sovereign-wealth funds (SWFs) swallowing prized assets around the world, such as Abu Dhabi Investment Authority (ADIA) and the Kuwait Investment Authority acquiring billionaire stakes in Citigroup.

In November 2008, the International Energy Agency (IEA) released the most important report in its three-decade history, *World Energy Outlook 2008*. Executive director Nobuo Tanaka summed it all up: "The era of cheap oil is over. Current trends in energy supply and consumption are patently unsustainable—environmentally, economically and socially—they can and must be altered." The consequences are stark; as cheap oil was the basis of

20th century industrialization, the economy of the 21st century will have to be ... something completely different.

According to the report, current oil-field production is declining by 9% a year. Even with ultra high-tech methods, the decline would still be 6.7% a year. Tanaka stressed, "Even if oil demand was to remain flat to 2030, 45 million barrels per day of gross capacity—roughly four times the current capacity of Saudi Arabia—would need to be built by 2030 just to offset the effect of oil-field decline." Translation: before 2030, just to keep running, the global economy will have to replace almost 60% of the oil it is currently producing.

The IEA advanced a few scenarios for oil to be replaced—all of them controversial and expensive. Nevertheless, the Obama presidency would really break exceptional ground if it frontally addressed some measure of change in the single greatest vector of oil guzzling in the whole world: the one-passenger U.S. auto (and SUV) culture. That would mean a massive cultural revolution: extensive investments in public transport and extensive promotion of carpooling and, of course, walking would cut the waste by half.

Meanwhile, the world will keep running the risk of ripping itself apart in the mad scramble for remaining oil and gas reserves. This mad scramble may be the defining aspect of Liquid War. The risk of Pipelineistan wars is being constantly increased by both U.S. and China flooding African oil-rich states like Angola, Nigeria and Sudan with weapons (U.S. corporate media never mentions that the Chinese-led oil industry in Sudan is at the mercy of guerrillas in both the South and in Darfur) as well as blatantly interfering in the Caspian basin, from Azerbaijan to Kazakhstan.

In this mad global scramble for energy, the case of Rising China vs. the U.S. is paramount.

Political economy master and professor of Sociology at Johns Hopkins University Giovanni Arrighi identifies what he calls "three plan Bs" the U.S. had to deal with China. 1) a relentless Cold War throughout the global perimeter. 2) Accommodation—through a Kissingerian strategy of cooptation. 3) A "happy" option; the U.S. sits back, sells weapons and watches while other powers fight. That's what the U.S. did to Europe in the first half of the 20th century.

Arrighi stresses China won't be an aggressive power—it comes from a different tradition in international relations; while Europe was devoured by endless intestinal wars, China enjoyed 500 years of peace. When the U.S. established world domination, it did what the Chinese had been doing for centuries: distribute gifts. Arrighi identifies "how to relate to the various U.S. plan Bs for China" as the central question of the 21st century.

Slovenian philosophy bad boy Slavoj Zizek should also be bedside reading for President Obama. Zizek drives home the point that China cannot be reduced to a "good guys vs. bad guys" scenario. He argues provocatively that one of the key reasons the West demonizes China is "ideological: Tibetan Buddhism, deftly propagated by the Dalai Lama, is one of the chief points of reference for the hedonist New Age spirituality... Tibet has become a mythic entity onto which we project our dreams." Just as—cynics would argue—Obama during the 2008 campaign became a mythic savior entity onto which his supporters projected their dreams.

Zizek also doubts that after the explosion of Chinese capitalism (or "market socialism," as the Little Helmsman Deng Xiaoping defined it; or perhaps "non-capitalist market society," as Arrighi puts it) democracy would assert itself "as capital's 'natural' political form of organization." After all, "the weird combination of capitalism and communist rule proved not to be a ridiculous paradox, but a blessing. China has developed so fast not in spite of authoritarian communist rule, but because of it."

And that leads us to a delightful paradox (maybe not in the Beltway). What if democracy "never arrives?" Zizek entertains "the suspicion that [China's] authoritarian capitalism is not merely a reminder of our past—of the process of capitalist accumulation which, in Europe, took place from the 16th to the 18th century—but a sign of our future ...What if the combination of the Asian knout and the European stock market proves economically more efficient than liberal capitalism? What if democracy, as we understand it, is no longer the condition and motor of economic development, but an obstacle to it?"

Definitely the stuff of many a white night at the White House.

2B. ENTER THE SCO

Even before 9/11 China had formulated its own response to the renewed, slow, reptilian encroachment by the West represented by the NATO armies: the Shanghai Cooperation Organization (SCO), founded in June 2001, which among its multi-layered economic-military-regional cooperation roles should also function as a sort of security belt around Afghanistan. The SCO is virtually unmentioned by the bulk of this very strict apparatus of public opinion control—U.S. corporate media.

Iran is a crucial part of West Asia. As it is identified by the intelligentsia from Tehran and Delhi to Beijing and Moscow, a hypothetical war on Iran—still the ultimate wet dream of Dick "Angler" Cheney and his neo-con chamberlains and comrades-in-arms—would be a war not only against the SCO's Russia and China, but against the whole of Asia.

China essentially dreams of a secure, fast-flowing New Silk Road from the Caspian to Xinjiang, its Far West. Iran, India and Pakistan currently enjoy observer status at the SCO. One of the SCO's stated aims is to be able to protect Pipelineistan in all directions. This is what the Washington ruling elite would like NATO to do not only in Europe but across Eurasia. This is what Russia and China want the SCO to do across Asia. A clash is, of course, inevitable.

The SCO should be understood, as Chinese intelligentsia sees it, as an alliance of five non-Western civilizations—Russian, Chinese, Muslim, Hindu, and Buddhist. Take that, Samuel "civilization clash" Huntington. In the minds of the collective leadership in Beijing the SCO holds the possibility of evolving into the basis of a collective security system in Eurasia and to decisively influence global security—much to the discomfort of informed strategists Zbig Brzezinski and Brent Scowcroft.

At the moment the SCO is keeping what it calls a "6+4" format (6 member-countries plus 4 countries with observer status). Their territories make up no less than 3/5 of Eurasia, holding 25% of the global population (or the majority of it if the populations of observer countries are considered), a fabulous wealth of natural resources, and some of the world's fastest growing economies, even in times of crisis.

The Chinese see the new world order as being determined by the BRIC countries' quadrangle —Brazil, Russia, China, and India—plus a hopefully reunified triangle of Islam—Iran, Saudi Arabia, and Turkey—and a unified South America, all to be eventually related to the SCO.

Already in 1999 the Chinese saw NATO aggressively expanding into the Balkans and identified this new game for what it was: an energy war, where the Empire of U.S. military bases (represented by Camp Bondsteel) met Pipelineistan (represented by the AMBO pipeline).

The wily Russians had even beaten the Chinese to the punch, via their Defense Ministry International Military Cooperation Department, which worked on this security dossier alongside then Russian Deputy Foreign Minister G. Karasin, and supported by notorious pragmatist Cold Warrior, former KGB General and former Prime Minister Yevgeny Primakov. The Russian project was subsequently frozen, but their ideas were the embryo of the SCO.

This is how the Russians framed the SCO ideology:

> "The unipolar world order is unstable, perilous for mankind, and prone to dictatorship based on military power";

> "The global dominance of the liberal market model can result in a global economic imbalance, an intensification of the struggle over natural resources, and mass extinction due to famine and armed conflicts";

> "The philosophy of the prosperity limited to the 'golden billion' is unacceptable to mankind as it destroys harmony between humans and nature and causes civilization clashes" [this is a critique of Western projections according to which 20% of the world's population is enough to keep the global economy running].

Thus the Russians proposed:

> "To establish a second pole of global power with the life philosophy and attitude to environment different from those in

the West, a pole assigning greater priority to spiritual and moral values, to collectivist tendencies";

"To harmonize the relations between countries and civilizations";

"To create a security system based on a balance of powers."

Years later, does the Chinese intelligentsia disagree with all this? Far from it.

Interrogated by the *People's Daily*, Sun Zhuangzhi, a scholar at the Social Sciences Research Center in Beijing said Russia's "attitude is most of all due to their renewed power, they will not be in a subordinate position," as well as due to a rampant nationalist sentiment. He did not fail to mention the renewed impetus of the SCO, which has given "a new dimension to the strategic cooperation" between China and Russia.

For his part Shen Jiru, a professor of political economy at the elite Chinese Academy of Social Sciences stressed, "It is imperative for Russia to clearly affirm its opposition to a unipolar world. Drawing lessons from history," he argues, Russia is not engaging in a new Cold War, but wants an equal partnership with the West. Sounds like the current, official Russian President Dmitry Medvedev's platform.

And how does China fit into Russia's political strategy? Wang Zhengquan, professor at Renmin Daxue University's Institute of International Relations, once again stresses "Russia needs Chinese help to recover its great power status and counter the U.S.'s strategy of world domination." He describes the Russian strategy as "measured attacks" trying to pierce the "wall" designed by the U.S. and the EU to box Russia in.

2C. KOSOVO: A PIPELINEISTAN WAR

In myriad ways, Kosovo in February 2008 became the new Kurdistan (and the other way around), as much as Iraq, fighting a Turkish threat from the north, risked becoming the new Yugoslavia.

The unilateral independence of Kosovo had nothing to do with "democracy." The point of this NATO provocation towards Vladimir Putin's Russia—a historic ally of Serbia—revolved around two crucial, interrelated facts on the ground: Pipelineistan and the empire of 737 (and counting) U.S. military bases in 130 countries operated by 350,000-plus Americans. In short: it revolved around the trans-Balkan AMBO pipeline and Camp Bondsteel in Kosovo, the largest U.S. base built in Europe in a generation.

It laid bare a stark "continuity" from the Bill Clinton to the George W. Bush administrations. Yugoslavia and Iraq also "taught" the world two lessons. From Clinton's humanitarian imperialism to Bush's "war on terror," it has always been a matter of exclusive Washington prerogative. Blowback, of course, as Putin himself warned, would be inevitable. The question is: will an Obama presidency break this pattern?

The 78-day, 1999 bombing of Yugoslavia, allegedly to dislodge a "new Hitler" (Slobodan Milosevic) was mirrored by the 2003 "shock and awe" bombing of Iraq, to dislodge another "new Hitler" (Saddam Hussein). Clinton, demonizing the Serbs, used NATO to sidestep the lack of a U.N. mandate; Bush, also without a U.N. mandate, demonized Iraqis and went all the way with just an authorization by the U.S. Congress.

Clinton attacked the former Yugoslavia to expand post-Cold War NATO right up to the borders of the former Soviet Union. Bush attacked Iraq to seize the "Big Prize" (per Dick Cheney) in energy resources. Militarization and hegemonic control were at the heart of both operations. Yugoslavia was devastated, fragmented, balkanized and ethnically cleansed into mini-countries. Iraq was devastated, fragmented, pushed towards balkanization and towards ethnic cleansing along sectarian and religious lines.

Obama's Secretary of State, Hillary Clinton, considered Yugoslavia's balkanization and Kosovo's independence (amputation of Serbia, rather) as "democracy" and a "successful" accomplishment of U.S. foreign policy.

This "model" new independent state saluted at the time by the U.S., Germany, France and Britain—and virtually no one else—is, according to Vladimir Ovtchinky, a criminologist and former head of Interpol's Russia bureau during the 1990s, "a mafia state in the heart of Europe." It's basically run by Hashim Thaci, a former Marxist who later embraced a nationalist socialism with criminal overtones as one of the youngest chiefs of the UCK (the Kosovo Liberation Army), operating under the codename "The Serpent."

Madeleine Albright, then U.S. Secretary of State, pushed "The Serpent" into the limelight when she attributed to him "the brightest future" among those Kosovars who were "fighting for democracy." Albright is back to being a bright star in Obama's foreign policy firmament.

The UCK was roughly a sort of Balkan al-Qaeda on heavy drugs— propped up enthusiastically by U.S. and British intelligence. British Special Forces trained the UCK in northern Albania while Turkish and Afghan military instructors taught them guerrilla tactics. Even Osama bin Laden had been in Albania, in 1994; al-Qaeda had a solid UCK connection.

Writing in the Russian daily *Ogoniok*, Ovtchinky described how Albanian Kosovar clans always controlled opium and then heroin trafficking from Afghanistan and Pakistan through the Balkans towards Western Europe; then during the late 1990s a 3% tax started to finance all UCK operations. The UCK benefited from more than 750 million euros in drug money to buy weapons.

According to Interpol and Europol, just in 1999 and 2000, these Kosovar mafias made no less than 7.5 billion euros—also by diversifying from narco-smuggling into human trafficking and large-scale prostitution. In Germany, they made a killing in Kalashnikov trafficking and fake euro banknotes. And as late as in 2007, Italy's top three mafias—the Cosa Nostra, the Camorra and Ndrangheta—were seriously thinking of creating a unified cartel to face the ultra-heavy Albanian Kosovar mafia.

The core of the self-described "international community" applauding Kosovo's independence was caught in silent-scream mode when confronted with the possibility of independence for Flanders in Belgium, northern Cyprus, the Serbian Republic of Bosnia, the Basque country in Spain, Gibraltar, Indian Kashmir (the Jammu & Kashmir Liberation Front, JKLF, started to make some rumblings), Tibet, Taiwan, Abkahzia and South Ossetia (both in Georgia and both Russia-friendly), Palestine and Kurdistan. Northern Kosovo itself—totally Serbian-populated—and western Macedonia also don't qualify to become independent. So why

Kosovo? Enter the AMBO pipeline and Camp Bondsteel—Pipelineistan meets the U.S. Empire of Bases.

AMBO is short for Albanian Macedonian Bulgarian Oil Corp, an entity registered in the U.S. The $1.1 billion AMBO pipeline (also known as the Trans-Balkan), supposed to be finished by 2011, will get oil brought from the Caspian to a terminal in Georgia and then by tanker through the Black Sea to the Bulgarian port of Burgas, and relay it through Macedonia to the Albanian port of Vlora.

Clinton's NATO war against Yugoslavia and pro-Albania was thus crucial to secure Vlora's strategic location. The oil will then be shipped to Rotterdam in the Netherlands and refineries on the U.S. West Coast, thus bypassing the ultra-congested Bosphorus Strait and the Aegean and the Mediterranean seas.

The original AMBO feasibility study, as early as 1995, and then updated in 1999, is by a British subsidiary of Halliburton, Brown and Root Energy Services. AMBO totally fit into Dick Cheney's (and before him, Clinton's energy secretary Bill Richardson's) U.S. energy security grid. It's all about go-for-broke militarization of the crucial energy corridor from the Caspian through the Balkans, and about trying to isolate or sabotage both Russia and Iran.

Halliburton had to have a deeper hand in the whole scheme, and that's where Camp Bondsteel fits in—the largest overseas U.S. military base built since the Vietnam War. Bondsteel, built by Halliburton subsidiary Kellogg, Brown and Root on 400 hectares of farmland near the Macedonian border in southern Kosovo, is a sort of larger—and friendlier—five-star Guantanamo, with perks like Thai massage and loads of junk food. According to Chalmers Johnson in *The Sorrows of Empire*, "army wags say facetiously that there are only two man-made objects that can be seen from outer space—the Great Wall of China and Camp Bondsteel." Bondsteel also doubles as Kosovo's Abu Ghraib—the largest prison in the "independent" entity, where prisoners can be held indefinitely without charges pressed and without defense attorneys. If Obama is serious about closing down Guantanamo he would have to do the same with Kosovo's Bondsteel.

Kosovo's "independence" had been brewing since 1999. A single 1999 photo tells the whole story—establishing beyond doubt those elusive "international community" ties. The photo unites Hashim Thaci, then head of terrorist outfit UCK and current prime minister of Kosovo; Bernard Kouchner, then UN administrator of Kosovo and current French Foreign Minister in the Sarkozy administration; Sir Mike Jackson, then commander of NATO's occupying force and current consultant for a Blackwater-style mercenary outfit; and general Wesley Clark, then NATO supreme commander and now a close military adviser to Hillary Clinton.

Iraqi Kurds are still tempted to believe Kosovo is a meaty precedent pointing to the emergence of an independent Iraqi Kurdistan—their dream, and Turkey's nightmare. Just as in Kosovo, Pipelineistan is at play (centered around the fabulous energy wealth of Kirkuk); and Iraqi Kurdistan, since 1991, had been a sort of extended Camp Bondsteel anyway, an American-protected enclave in Saddam's Iraq and then a haven of stable "democracy" in Bush-devastated Iraq.

Kosovo's "internationally supervised independence" has nothing to do with autonomy. Amputated from Serbia, "liberated" Kosovo is no more than an EU (and NATO) protectorate, a neocolonial exercise with a viceroy and no say whatsoever over foreign policy. Think of "liberated" Iraq under the infamous Coalition Provisional Authority (CPA) run by viceroy L Paul Bremer. No wonder then Russian Foreign Minister Sergei Lavrov characterized Kosovo's independence as the beginning of the end of contemporary Europe.

As for Bondsteel, it's like a giant aircraft carrier, exercising surveillance not only over the Balkans but also over Turkey and the Black Sea (the new interface between the Euro-Atlantic community and the Greater Middle East, according to neo-con credo). Once again: will the Obama presidency be willing—or able —to revert a balkanization strategy that ultimately implies control of the Balkans themselves, the Middle East and Central Asia? Obama could start by questioning British Islamologist Bernard Lewis, an icon for the neo-cons, who contributed the conceptual framework.

2D. Georgia: a Pipelineistan war

The balance of power in Eurasia changed forever in August 9, 2008, at the break of the Georgia-Russia war. It boggles the mind that ultra high-tech U.S. intelligence could not have identified what the Russians had identified—the Georgians about to attack South Ossetia. The Red Army was more than ready to deliver a full-spectrum smackdown.

As Russian army colonel Igor Konashenko told Mark Ames of *Radar* magazine in a desert street corner of Tskhinvali, the capital of South Ossetia: "Twelve Georgian battalions invaded Tskhinvali, backed by columns of tanks, armored personal carriers, jets, and helicopters,' he says, happily waving at the wreckage, craters, and bombed-out buildings around us. 'You see how well they fought, with all their great American training—they abandoned their tanks in the heat of the battle and fled ... Everything that the Georgians left behind, I mean everything, was American. All the guns, grenades, uniforms, boots, food ration —they just left it all. Our boys stuffed themselves on the food. It was tasty." The fabulous booty also included 65 intact tanks crammed with state-of-the-art NATO, American and Israeli technology.

Once again, the scenario mixes NATO expansion, pushed by the U.S., with Pipelineistan. Bush senior (to Gorbachev) and Clinton (to Yeltsin) had promised that NATO would not expand into the former Soviet Union's sphere of influence. The promise was broken in 1998 (NATO expanded to Poland, Hungary and the Czech Republic), broken again in 2004 (expansion in Central Europe plus incorporation of the three Baltic states), and set to be broken again in 2008 with the possibility of incorporating Georgia and Ukraine. The Kremlin could not but identify it for what it is: strategic encirclement (St. Petersburg used to be 1,200 miles away from NATO; now Estonia is only 60 miles away). NATO in this case did or could not "save" Georgia for a simple reason: in Pipelineistan logic, the Middle East—and crucially Iran—is way more crucial than the Caucasus.

Israel for its part had big stakes going in the Georgia-Russia war. *DEBKAfile* reported how Israel had been actively negotiating with Georgia, Azerbaijan, Turkey and Turkmenistan to have access to oil and gas pumped to the Turkish Mediterranean port of Ceyhan and then to Israel's oil terminal at Ashkelon and the Red Sea port of Eilat, from which Israel could make a killing selling oil to Asia via the Indian Ocean. That explains over a thousand Israeli military advisers training Georgians in commando, air, sea, and armored and artillery combat tactics. The Red Army, of course, made minced meat of these trainees.

What was not reported in the fog of war was how the demagogic, hot headed Columbia-educated lawyer and Georgian President Mikhail Saakashvili—who climbed to power on top of the 2003 CIA-conducted Rose Revolution largely financed by George Soros, and had been advised by John McCain's foreign policy guru, mega lobbyst Randy Scheunemann—was a Zbig Brzezinski creation to begin with. As for Obama's brand of diplomacy in response to the war, it was not exactly encouraging, considering the challenges his presidency will face. He talked to Saakashvili, to Bush's National Security Council, arguably to his mentor Zbig, but he did not talk to anybody in Moscow. And then Obama started toeing the Bush line. In a statement quoted by the *New York Times*, Obama got it all wrong: "What is clear is that Russia has invaded Georgia's sovereign—has encroached on Georgia's sovereignty."

Georgia anyway remains an absolutely key node in Washington's energy policy in the Caucasus and Central Asia—because of a larger than life obsession: bypassing Iran. In the event the Obama presidency would change the overall game plan that would be a geopolitical event of earth-shaking proportions.

Slightly over 10 years ago, then Halliburton CEO Dick Cheney said

> *"I can't think of a time when we've had a region emerge as suddenly to become as strategically significant as the Caspian."*

The Caspian wet dreams remain—and they have not exactly been restricted to the Cheney camp.

As I have detailed in *Globalistan*, the $4 billion Baku-Tbilisi-Ceyhan (BTC) pipeline—sold to the Azerbaijani elite by Zbig Brzensiki in Baku in 1995—and running from the Sangachal Terminal half-an-hour south of Baku and across Georgia to the Marine Terminal in the Turkish port of Ceyhan on the Mediterranean, is a 1,767 km-long, 44 m wide pipeline that represents the perfect marriage between Pipelineistan and Liquid War. It is useful to remember that the pipeline straddles no less than six war zones, ongoing or potential: Nagorno-Karabakh (an Armenian enclave in Azerbaijan); Chechnya and Dagestan (both in Russia); South Ossetia and Abkhazia (both in Georgia); and Turkish Kurdistan.

It was essentially the U.S. Israel lobby, in its burning desire to reward Turkey for its close diplomatic and military relations, that managed to pressure Washington into conceiving an alternative route, through Turkey and bypassing Iran, to bring oil from Azerbaijan to the Mediterranean. A Baku-Tehran-Khark (BTK) pipeline could have been built for next to nothing compared to BTC—as it would bypass both unstable Georgia and Kurdish-populated eastern Anatolia.

BTC has to be watched absolutely non-stop to prevent bombing or sabotage. This actually happens in the James Bond movie *The World is not Enough*, a huge hit with geopolitical junkies, where sexy nuclear scientist Denise Richards disarms a fake nuclear bomb inside the pipeline (just to deliver a "realist" counterpoint, Russia bombed a few stretches near the pipeline's route during the Russia-Georgia war). In the Bond flick, a wicked Azeri heiress (played by the breathtaking Sophie Marceau) "owns" the pipeline, which happens to mirror the exact route of BTC.

Even though the Russians never planned to occupy Georgia, or to take over BTC, Alfa Bank oil and gas analyst Konstantin Batunin has stressed the Russia-Georgia war proved to global investors Georgia is simply not reliable as an energy transit country—a key node in Pipelineistan.

Azerbaijan for its part was the only success story in U.S.-driven Pipelineistan. Bill Clinton, advised by Brzezinski, literally "stole" Baku from Russia's "near abroad" by promoting BTC. But Baku fully understood the new writing on the wall in the Caucasus after the Russia-Georgia war, and is now allowing itself to be seduced by Russia again. To top it off, Azerbaijan President Ilham Aliyev (the real life counterpart to Sophie Marceau in the Bond flick) simply can't stand Saakashvili, who made Azerbaijan lose at least $500 million when Caucasus Pipelineistan was shut down because of the war.

Russia's seduction blitzkrieg in Central Asia revolves around offering to buy Kazakh, Uzbek and Turkmen gas at European prices. The Russians offered the same deal to the Azeris in the southern Caucasus. Baku not only loved the idea; it is now negotiating with Russia more capacity for the Baku-Novorossiisk pipeline while deciding to pump less oil for BTC and the Baku-Supsa pipeline.

Obama needs to understand the dire implications. Less Azeri oil on BTC (its full capacity is 1 million barrels a day, mostly shipped to Europe) means the pipeline goes broke, which is exactly what Russia wants.

The U.S. "bypassing Russia and Iran" obsession manifests itself in myriad other ways. ChevronTexaco run the monster Tengiz oil field in Kazakhstan. Pipelineistan moves the oil to Novorossiisk, in the Russian Black Sea; and another rail link to the Black Sea goes to the Georgian port of Batumi. Kashagan, the monster oil field in the northeast Caspian, is still being developed. In the southern Caspian, BP runs the Azeri-Chirag-Gunashli field. Not only the Iranians, anyone in Pipelineistan knows the cheapest and fastest way to let all this oil flow would be through Iran.

The Kazakhs want a 900-mile, $1.2 billion pipeline from Tengiz to Belek on the eastern Caspian and then to the Iranian port of Khark, on the Persian Gulf, passing through Tehran, Qom and Isfahan. Washington has moved mountains to block it.

The French giant TotalFinaElf, allied with the National Iranian Oil Company (NIOC), also wants a pipeline from Kashagan across the Caspian to Iran, linked with another pipeline across Iran to the Persian Gulf. And the Russians, via their Transneft, allied with the Kazakhs from KazTransOil, want a pipeline linking Omsk, in Siberia, with Iran's port of Neka on the Caspian. This would have been a particular crucial Pipelineistan node, as Russians, Turkmen and Kazakhs could swap their crude for Iranian oil in terminals on the Persian Gulf (Iran and Central Asia already engage in oil-swapping, although in much smaller amounts). But Washington blocked it.

What Washington wanted was for the Kazakhs to build a trans-Caspian pipeline from Aktau to Baku, linking the fabulous reserves of Kashagan with BTC. That would have caused an environmental disaster of monumental proportions. At least in this particular case, it was the Russians and the Iranians who killed it.

Kashagan itself—the absolute jewel in the Caspian crown, with reserves of as many as 9 billion barrels—is a gigantic puzzle, typical of byzantine Pipelineistan deal-making. It is operated by a consortium of Western majors led by Italy's ENI. Individual companies like ENI, Royal Dutch Shell, ConocoPhillips, Japan's Inpex and Kazakhstan's KazMunaiGas control different phases of production and shipping.

As usual in Pipelineistan the question is which routes will deliver Kashagan oil to the world after the production starting date in 2013. This spells, of course, Liquid War. Wily Kazakh President Nazarbayev would like to use the Russian-controlled Caspian Pipeline Consortium (CPC) to pump Kashagan crude to the Russians in the Black Sea. CPC itself is another puzzle—Russia holds a 24% stake in partnership with Chevron, Royal Dutch Shell and ExxonMobil.

The Kazakhs have all the cards in their hands. Their best play is to wait for another major Russian gambit in Pipelineistan—the East Siberia to the Pacific (ESPO) pipeline—in 2012 and then sell most of the oil to Asia (a staggering 150 million tons a year by 2015). According to the Russian Energy Ministry KazTransOil has its eyes set on ESPO. The big winner in this case? China, of course.

How oil will flow from Kashagan will decide if BTC—once hyped by Washington as the ultimate Western escape route from dependence on oil from the Persian Gulf—lives or dies. In her last visit to Kazakhstan, on which she is supposed to be an expert, former U.S. Secretary of State Condoleeza Rice tried to put the best face on a dire situation, saying

"This is not some kind of contest for the affection of Kazakhstan between the countries of the region."

But just like Azerbaijan, Kazakhstan saw which way the wind is blowing; Nazarbayev supported Russia against Georgia. And Nazarbayev himself delivered the clincher, even before Rice's arrival in Astana:

"I personally was a witness to the fact that Georgia attacked first. I was in Beijing on August 8 with Mr. Putin, when we first heard the news. I think the coverage of those events was biased. Whoever you may blame for the conflict, the facts are bad enough."

2E. THE IRANIAN ANGLE

As I stressed in *Globalistan*, Iranian officials and analysts identify a total "interdependence of Asia and Persian Gulf geo-ecopolitics."

It boils down to Asian integration with a sprawling Pipelineistan linking the Persian Gulf, Central Asia, South Asia and China. The major Iranian card in the game is the gigantic South Pars field—responsible for at least 9% of the world's proven gas reserves.

Iran, as well as China and Russia, see a hypothetical U.S. attack as a war against the Asian Energy Security Grid. A major node of the grid will be the $ 7.6 billion Iran-Pakistan-India (IPI) pipeline, also known as the "Peace Pipeline." After years of wrangling, an agreement for its construction was signed in 2008. In this case, both Pakistan and India have mirrored each other by standing up to relentless Washington pressure.

Pakistan is a desperate customer of the Asian Energy Security Grid. By April 2008, then President Pervez Musharraf, in a speech at Beijing's Tsinghua University, was virtually begging China to invest in Pipelineistan, link the Persian Gulf and Pakistan with China's Far West, and thus help Pakistan become an "energy corridor" to the Middle East.

One of the big developments of 2008 is that Iran has become a gas-exporting country. By March 2008, Iran was demanding to be a full partner in the SCO. There were problems from the beginning. Tajikistan was in favor. Kazakhstan was against it—because of Iran's "unpredictability." China was discreet. Russia was pragmatic. Military analyst Anatoly Tsyganok told the website *ferghana.ru* "this would allow Moscow and Beijing to better control Tehran": but as Middle East expert Vladimir Sajin stressed, the process would take time, because "even Russia and China have recently been more forceful towards Tehran because of its nuclear enrichment program." Everything in the SCO presupposes a consensus between Russia and China.

Iran's relations with both Russia and China are excellent—and will remain so whoever is elected as the new Iranian President in the summer of 2009. China desperately needs Iranian oil and gas, and has plenty of weapons and cheap consumer goods to sell. Russia wants to sell more weapons and nuclear energy technology—not to mention it needs Iran's cooperation to finally define the status of the Caspian (Is it a sea? It it a lake?) so Caspian energy wealth can be exploited smoothly. During the Bush disaster years Russia had the best of both worlds regarding Iran— profiting from the West's demonization to conduct plenty of business.

Now there's some sort of endgame in the charts. By the end of 2008 there was a strong buzz in Moscow that President Mahmoud Ahmadinejad will be "on his way out" in the 2009 Iranian presidential elections. That would mean a new U.S. President and a new, more pragmatist Iranian President able to conduct a dialogue. Turkey—a key regional power for both the U.S. and EU, with vastly improved relations with Iran—had already identified the opening by mid-2008. And Obama himself could not have failed to identify the positioning of Turkey as the real and metaphorical bridge between the Christian and Muslim worlds.

In Pipelineistan terms, only a fully normalized U.S./EU relationship with Iran would lead to the success of Nabucco—the strategy privileged by the U.S. to reduce Western Europe's energy dependence on Russian energy. Pipelineistan carrying Iranian gas to Europe has to go through Turkey.

Obama must have read the signs. The Iranian leadership "calmed down" the Lebanese cauldron; told the Shi'ite Mahdi Army of Muqtada al-

Sadr to back down in Iraq; supported the deal between Hamas and Israel; approved a U.S. diplomatic presence in Tehran; approved the ideas of non-stop, direct flights between the U.S. and Iran.

But there are a lot of caveats. In one of his summer of 2008 Friday prayer speeches at the University of Tehran, former President and uber-pragmatist Akbar Hashemi Rafsanjani more or less laid down the law:

"The Israeli lobby in the U.S. is once again working hard to torpedo nuclear talks by harping on a 'deadline' and an 'ultimatum' to Iran."

"With patience and perseverance, let us give this negotiation a chance. Every time the situation is about to improve, these Western hardliners and radicals begin their diversionary ploys, which only shows some powers cannot bear to see peace in the region."

"Iran is ready to negotiate. The aim of the talks is also clear ... Staging military maneuvers and holding talks from a distance cannot resolve issues. Do not try to invent pretexts. Be patient and let wise people sit down and talk to resolve the problems."

2F. When NATO meets Pipelineistan

At virtually every recent NATO summit Washington has been ordering NATO to protect Pipelineistan. This spells the obvious: reluctant Europeans being dragged into possibly devastating energy wars—Pipelineistan meets the "war on terror." It didn't happen during the Russia-Georgia war, but it is already happening, for instance, in Afghanistan (where a pipeline has not even been built).

Pipelineistan Europe could be resumed by a formula: Nabucco vs. South Stream. Once again, it's a question of how to bypass Russia.

For this to happen, Europe desperately needs Central Asia. A measure of how Europe will try anything to unlock Central Asia was provided by an EU-Central Asian forum in Ashgabat, Turkmenistan, in April 2008.

This forum was designed and lobbied by Germany. In Berlin's point of view, the European Central Asian strategy means "security"—which means choosing from a basket of energy export routes. This inevitably translates into a Brussels-style bureaucratic alphabet soup, namely TRACECA (Europe-Caucasus-Asia transport corridor) and INOGATE (oil and gas export to Europe). Its real life translation is the perennially troubled Trans-Caspian gas pipeline. Russia, of course, is totally anti-Trans-Caspian.

Dosym Satpayev of the Kazakh Risk Evaluation Group told the website *ferghana.ru* he suspects the only thing Europe cares about is energy. But he also pointed out Robert Simmons, NATO secretary general's special envoy for security matters, and his constant Central Asian tours. So is it oil and gas, is it NATO expansion, or both? Andrei Grozin, head of the Department of Central Asia and Kazakhstan of the Institute of CIS Countries, went straight to the point, faithfully reflecting the disarray in the corridors of Brussels: "The Europeans themselves admit that the strategy they have at this point is but a transition period document." This fateful document has been at the center of endless white nights in Brussels.

Satpayev argues—correctly—that in a mad scramble involving Moscow, Brussels and of course Washington, the real winner is, once again, China: "Its military influence is secured by the SCO. The Atasu-Alashankou pipeline is working" [this crucial, $800 million Pipelineistan node was opened in December 2005 by Kazakhstan President Nazarbayev but still needs Russian crude from Western Siberia to reach its full annual capacity of 20 million tons by 2010].

Without even mentioning the gas deal of the century—$100 billion—between China and Iran, Satpayev added "gas pipelines to China from Turkmenistan and Kazakhstan via Uzbekistan are being built. China aspires for development of the fields in the Turkmen sector of the Caspian shelf and promises $900 million for other projects in Kyrgyzstan and Turkmenistan. Russia in the meantime has been doing nothing."

That would be an exaggeration. As we have already stressed, China badly needs Russian liquefied natural gas (LNG)—there have been furious negotiations since March 2006 when Gazprom chief executive Alexei Miller and Chen Geng, then head of China's CNPC, signed a memorandum of understanding for the delivery of LNG to China. Gas imports are a supremely vital matter of Chinese national security.

As in all matters Pipelineistan, it's a compound question of price and route. The 2,800 km-long western route, already being built on the Russian side, crosses the Altai. This crucial Altai pipeline will link the West Siberian fields with Xinjiang, China's Far West, and connect with China's West-East pipeline which finishes in Shanghai. But there's also an alternative eastern route, not yet subjected to a feasibility study, from Yakutia to northeastern China. Whatever route prevails, for Gazprom this is a windfall—Pipelineistan expanding to China is far shorter than to Europe, and there are no transit fees to be paid. So as a gas supplier to China, Russia would theoretically win over Pipelineistan coming from Iran or Turkmenistan.

Russian LNG starts flowing into China from Sakhalin-2, at the southern end of Sakhalin island, in 2009 (Gazprom took over control of the project from Royal Dutch Shell in 2008). Not only China is being supplied—Japan, South Korea and even the U.S. are in the mix. Sakhalin-1, operated by ExxonMobil, may also supply China. But the decision is Gazprom's. Gazprom told Exxon it wants the gas for the Russian market. But most of the gas could even end up supplying the U.S. market.

As New York University professor Nouriel Roubini has stressed in his *RGE Monitor* website, up to the summer of 2008 Russia was growing at almost 8% a year, oil was at around $140 a barrel, there was an enormous fiscal and current account surplus, over $600 billion in foreign reserves, and widespread talk of turning the ruble into a major reserve currency, at least for the CIS bloc. The Russian financial peak was during the August 2008 war with Georgia. Then came the U.S.-generated global financial crisis and the dramatic slump in oil prices. Times in 2009 and 2010 will be tough for the Kremlin—a.k.a. the Gazprom nation.

But none of these contingencies will derail the Kremlin's desire to forge a Central Asian energy club within the SCO—basically as a way to promote an energy entente cordiale with China. Russian Deputy Industry and Energy Minister Ivan Materov has been among those insistently denying this would be a mini-OPEC within the SCO. Spy vs. spy addicts are overexcited anticipating if, and how, the Obama presidency will throw a spanner in these Sino-Russian works. It boils down to how the Obama presidency will counteract the so far extremely successful Russian strategy: to undermine by all possible means the U.S.-promoted east-west Caspian energy corridor, and solidify instead a Russian-controlled Pipelineistan stretching from Kazakhstan to Greece and the whole of Western Europe.

Only a few days after the EU called an emergency summit in Brussels to discuss the dire consequences of the war in the Caucasus, Moscow may have hardly expected that they would include a new push for the frantically U.S.-encouraged Nabucco pipeline.

In mid-September 2008 the Presidents of Poland, the Czech Republic, Slovakia and Hungary got together in the small town of Piestany, Slovakia to forcefully urge the EU to cut its dependency on Russian energy. And in an extraordinary plot twist, both Azerbaijan and Turkmenistan decided to support Nabucco at a forum in Baku. Even Russia's South Stream partners Greece and Hungary decided to hedge their bets. And to top it off, Iranian Oil Minister Gholam Hossein Nozari told the *Wiener Zeitung* newspaper "clearly, Nabucco cannot be implemented without Iran. The country with 16 percent of the world's gas reserves cannot be ignored. But we cannot wait forever, so Austria needs to hurry. The EU needs Iran."

So Russia still had not been able to close down Nabucco. Then there's another prized Gazprom offspring—the Nord Stream pipeline to Germany across the Baltic Sea floor. Nord Stream AG needs permission from transit countries. But Sweden, Denmark and Finland—all eagerly encouraged by Washington—are raising tons and tons of ecological restrictions.

Plot twists in Pipelineistan are worthy of the best science fiction.

Until then the last great upset had been in March 2008, when **Alexei Miler, the powerful head of Gazprom, was in for a rude shock: the three state gas companies in key Central Asian "stans"—Uzbekneftgaz, Turkmengaz and Kazmunaigaz—had told him that starting in 2009, they** will only sell their gas to Gazprom according to European rates. Gazprom, although with deep pockets, could have never expected that Uzbekistan, Turkmenistan and Kazakhstan would all gang up on it this way.

The new development seemed to totally revert the success of then-President Putin's visit to Kazakhstan and Turkmenistan in May 2007—when he made sure that prized Turkmen gas would arrive in Europe only through Kazakhstan and Russia.

But there would be yet another sensational plot twist. By May 2008, Russia again seemed sure to have secured a virtual distribution monopoly of Central Asia's gas Pipelineistan. The name of the game was the Prikaspiisky pipeline—which would flow the bulk of natural gas from Kazakhstan and Turkmenistan from the Caspian to Russia.

That's when the Chinese, according to Xinhua, started lobbying the Turkmen president, the spectacularly named Gurbanguly Berdymukhamedov, to speed up the construction of their own pipeline.

This Turkmen-Kazakh-China Pipelineistan node will be the longest and most expensive pipeline in the world—7,000 km at the most recent cost estimate of a staggering $26 billion, from eastern Turkmenistan to China's Guangdong province. The idea was first sketched as early as 1993. Only in April 2006 then Turkmen President, the flamboyant Saparmurad Niyazov signed a framework cooperation agreement in Beijing with Chinese President Hu Jintao. By July 2007, an agreement was signed between the Chinese National Petroleum Company (CNPC) and the responsible state agency of Turkmenistan, this time under Berdymukhamedov.

The absolute clincher is that for China, this massive geo-economic investment translates into a crucial geopolitical move. The 2007 agreement explicitly states that "Chinese interests" would not be "threatened from its [Turkmenistan's] territory by third parties." Translation: no Pentagon Empire of Bases allowed in Turkmenistan.

Putin had convinced the "stans" to play his game in 2007 just as an "anti-Russian energy summit," as dubbed by *Kommersant*, was taking place in Krakow, uniting Poland, Ukraine, Azerbaijan, Georgia and Kazakhstan itself.

These five countries somewhat agreed to build a new pipeline from Odessa to Gdansk, bypassing Russia, and part of the perennially troubled

Trans-Caspian pipeline. But the agreement was basically rhetorical. Poland wanted it to mean the beginning of an "energy NATO." It didn't work. Instead, Putin's key objective was reached—to reinforce Gazprom's iron clad position in an "energy dialogue" with the EU.

What's really taking place between Russia and the EU is more of a no-holds-barred energy war—Liquid War, in fact—than an energy dialogue. The EU and the U.S. pin all their hopes on the 3,300 km-long, $5.8 billion Nabucco pipeline, planned in 2004 and with construction about to start in 2009, already approved by the European Commission. Nabucco would transport Caspian Sea natural gas (potentially even from Iran, barring U.S. opposition) from Erzurum in Turkey to Baumgarten an der March in Austria via Bulgaria, Romania and Hungary.

In typical Pipelineistan fashion, Nabucco is owned by a consortium including Romania's Transgaz, Bulgaria's Bulgargaz, Austria's OMV, Turkey's Botas and MOL and Germany's RWE. France's Gaz de France was rejected by Turkey because France had recognized the Armenian genocide. Nabucco—perennially beset by financing problems—is the EU's preferential channel to not import natural gas only from Russia.

Russia's answer to Nabucco is the 1,200 km-long, $15 billion South Stream pipeline, carrying Siberian natural gas underground the Black Sea from Russia to Bulgaria. From Bulgaria, one branch would run south through Greece and southern Italy while the other would run north, through Serbia and Hungary towards northern Italy. The memorandum of understanding for South Stream was signed in Rome in June 2007 by Gazprom and Italy's ENI.

Up to the fall of 2008, it was very easy to see who was winning in the Nabucco vs South Stream war. In early January 2008, Bulgargaz spurned insistent EU siren calls for Nabucco and opted for South Stream—despite the fact that Bulgaria is both a EU and NATO member. Then Serbia also came on board—with Gazprom taking a 51% stake in NIS, the Serbian oil monopoly.

Nabucco is hardly a solution for Europe, for a number of key reasons. Will the EU be able to buy Iranian gas via Nabucco? Will the "stans" have enough gas to supply both Russia and China? Will they renege on their deals with Gazprom? Or will they keep rising their prices to Gazprom ad infinitum?

Turkmenistan, for instance, pledged to sell 50 billion cubic meters a year to Gazprom; it also has to provide 30 billion cubic meters for a pipeline to China starting in 2009; and it needs to supply 30 billion cubic meters for Nabucco. Few believe it can export that much.

All these variables led Duma deputy speaker Valery Yazev to declare "the death of Nabucco." Reinhard Mitschek, the head of the Nabucco consortium, flatly disagreed, extolling its "future potential."

The European Commission has been trying forever to seduce Turkmenistan to deliver gas to Europe—with scant success. Instead, the first gas to flow through Nabucco to Europe will probably be from Azerbaijan's Shah Deniz field. Then, in the best of possible worlds, it could even be gas from Iraq, according to Christian Dolezal, spokesperson for the Vienna-based Nabucco Gas Pipeline International GmbH.

Bulgaria, deciding to go the Gazprom way, definitely split up the EU amalgamation. Italy also went the Gazprom way. Putin touched the heart of the matter in late February 2008, while he was still president: "Our partners should do a very simple thing: they should take a calculator and see what is more profitable."

Those outside of the Beltway who advocate common sense in U.S. foreign policy expect that Obama will notice it: relentless Washington pressure to "sell" Nabucco to Europe on the grounds that it bypasses Russia is bound to be counter-productive. Russia will continue to do everything in its power to thwart it. It's the EU that must reach a common decision.

The U.S. itself depends on massive oil imports from Venezuela. But no EU members keep telling Washington what to do. The bottom line is that Europe needs everything—Nord Stream, South Stream and Nabucco. The bulk of the natural gas in all this Pipelineistan maze will be Russian anyway—and a substantial part may be Iranian, assuming the Obama presidency normalizes relations with Iran. There simply isn't enough gas in the market to fill Nabucco without Iran and Russia. For all the oil and gas wealth to be exploited in Central Asia, Russia and Iran still have more.

2G. IRAQ/IRAN

Nabucco spells classic Bush administration thinking: anything goes to bypass Russia. But in these high Pipelineistan stakes there was always an unspoken, invisible Iraqi angle as well.

Russia has not written Iraq off. Lukoil wants to convince Iraqi Oil Minister Hussain al-Shahristani to at least develop the giant West Qurna-2 oil field, which may hold up to 20 billion barrels and produce 1 million barrels of oil a day. Lukoil had signed a PSA in March 1997 with Saddam, which was to run until 2020, but then it became a victim of U.S. and UN-imposed sanctions. Saddam voided the contract at the end of 2002. Now Lukoil has a second chance.

All through 2008 the Bush administration was always dreaming—and pressuring—the Iraqi Parliament to approve its key "benchmark," the new Iraqi oil law which would in fact denationalize the Iraqi oil industry. Thus, in this best of possible Bush worlds, Iraqi gas, pumped through Syria, would be able to fill Nabucco, which would not be wholly dependent on the "stans." Meanwhile, there was always that far-fetched neo-con dream of regime change in Iran—enabling Iranian gas to reach Europe but under U.S. terms.

In the EU corridors everyone knows there's ultimately only one vector to make Nabucco commercially viable: Iran.

Iran became a gas exporter in 2008. But it cannot export more without tens of billion of dollars in foreign investment. Royal Dutch Shell and Repsol YPF of Spain already had to leave Iran under relentless Washington pressure. And French giant Total dropped out of developing phase 11 of giant South Pars, which lies beneath Iran and Qatar, one the world's largest natural gas fields which, according to Iran's Pars Special Economic Energy Zone, holds nearly 48% of Iran's total reserves. Total CEO Christophe de Margerie told the *Financial Times* "we would be taking too much political risk to invest in Iran because people will say: 'Total will do anything for money'."

The news did not affect Gazprom—which will develop "two or three" blocks of South Pars. And its daughter company, Gazpromneft, will also be part of a huge oil project in Iran. Gazprom has been firmly implanted in South Pars since 1997, alongside Total and Malaysia's Petronas.

Even Iran was not affected by the French drop out. Reza Kasaeizadeh, the managing director of Iran's NIOC, keeps insisting that Iran will supply no less than 10% of the world gas market in the next 20 years; currently it's only 1%. Iran at the moment exports gas only to Armenia and Turkey. When South Pars phases 17, 18 and 19 are developed by 2013 that will be a whole different ball game.

Even under severe U.S.-led sanctions, Iran is busy doing oil and gas deals with everybody and his neighbor—Malaysians, Indonesians, Syrians, Venezuelans, Chinese. And S.R. Kassaei Zadeh, managing director of NIOC is confident "we are going to India"—a reference to the ongoing push to finally get the so-called "Peace Pipeline" between Iran, Pakistan and India on track.

So will the Obama presidency follow the Bush administration and block foreign investment to pressure Iran over the nuclear dossier? Will the U.S. Congress insist on punishing foreign companies that invest more than $20 million in Iranian oil and gas projects?

Neighbors are taking no chances. The nearby Emirates would like to bypass the Persian Gulf altogether; Abu Dhabi is investing in a new 224-mile pipeline to be finished by 2010 to deliver oil at Oman ports, thus bypassing the Strait of Hormuz in the Persian Gulf. If the Strait of Hormuz is closed, the UAE economy melts down—something that never crossed the minds of neo-con armchair warriors. The new pipeline though will carry only 1.5 million barrels of oil a day. Another 1 million still has to be shipped through the Persian Gulf.

2H. IRAQ/AFGHANISTAN = PIPELINEISTAN

It was not about the "war on terror." It was not about weapons of mass destruction. It was not about "freedom and democracy to the Iraqi people," or to the "Afghan people." It was not about "Islamo-fascism." It certainly is about the Pentagon-coined "arc of instability" from the Middle East to Central Asia. And by July 2008 new evidence showed once again both Bush administration wars—in Afghanistan and Iraq—above all are about Pipelineistan.

Those were the days when the fateful words "war" and "oil" would never have been aligned in the same sentence anywhere in U.S. corporate media; the days when Donald Rumsfeld insisted Iraq had "literally nothing to do with oil."

But suddenly the U.S. and European Big Oil majors that controlled the Iraqi oil industry up to the 1972 nationalization—today represented by Exxon Mobil, Royal Dutch Shell, BP, Total and Chevron—seemed to be back with a vengeance. The *New York Times* duly redeemed itself from printing Ahmad Chalabi-fed WMD nonsense on its front page for months and actually engaged in news that's fit to print.

Thus the paper reported that "a group of American advisers led by a small State Department team played an integral part in drawing up contracts between the Iraqi government and five major Western oil companies to develop some of the largest fields in Iraq."

The bland language was misleading. This was no less than the first step in the de facto de-nationalization of the Iraqi oil industry—Dick Cheney's wet dream: a new round of immensely profitable oil deals, announced by Iraqi Oil Minister Sharistani, in which giants like Exxon Mobil can nail down long-term contracts and take away a large share of the oil from several massive operating fields like Rumaila and West Qurna.

Oil can be produced in these fields for a marginal cost of about one dollar a barrel, while its value on world markets at the time was around $140. The oil giants made their move seeking to bypass opposition in the

Iraqi Parliament and ignoring widespread suspicion and anger among the Iraqi public.

Hussein al-Shahristani, the Iraqi Oil minister, has always been a huge cheerleader of Big Oil taking over the Iraq oil industry. He dreams of Iraq as the world's second—or at least third-biggest—oil producer, competing with Saudi Arabia and Russia. To get there he is frantically selling out, trying to get voracious, predatory production sharing agreements (PSAs) over the heads of the Iraqi parliament and even harassing Iraqi oil unions.

At this early stage the whole thing is still about TSAs (technical support agreements); these are simple consultancy contracts to help Iraq raise its oil production by 500,000 barrels a day, not long-term contracts to develop juicy oil and gas fields.

But Iraqis were not fooled by the smoke and mirrors—nor by Big Oil hardball. At a press conference in Baghdad, Shahristani had to admit, "We did not finalize any agreement ... because they refused to offer consultancy based on fees, as they wanted a share of the oil." Big Oil, of course, wants the "Big Prize" (copyright Cheney).

What Cheney and Big Oil really want is to wallow in the extra-profitable 30-year PSAs once, and if, the new, IMF-redacted Iraqi oil law is forced through the gorges of the Iraqi Parliament, sealing a major U.S.-European takeover. This is what the U.S. power elite has always wanted.

Greg Muttit, co-director of the London-based oil industry research group Platform, explains that what's at stake at the current stage are "nine-year risk service contracts for six oil fields"; these are "halfway between TSAs and PSAs." Bids are due by March 2009, with signing in June 2009. As for the technical service contracts for five of the same oil fields, these are "no-bid contracts whose terms were dictated by the oil companies themselves." In other words: Big Oil is telling the Iraqi government what it wants.

And here's the catch. Muttit says, "The tendering of these fields is a big policy change, as producing fields were supposed to be developed by the Iraq National Oil Company [INOC], with only new fields allocated to foreign oil companies." Big Oil, though, wants the whole cake. INOC gets only a shabby 25% stake. Muttit makes an enlightening comparison with Libya, "where the national oil company gets around 80%, which is much more normal for fields of this size."

21. IPI VS. TAPI

By the summer of 2008 Bush/Cheney, unfazed by their own regime's death throes—and following what was already official policy under Clinton—were still poised to have one more crack at the new New Great Game in Central Asia, trying to thwart regional energy supremacy by both Russia and Iran.

In April 2008, Afghanistan, Turkmenistan, Pakistan and India signed a Gas Pipeline Framework Agreement, deciding—not for the first time—to build the $7.6 billion TAP (now TAPI) pipeline that would deliver natural gas from Turkmenistan to Pakistan and probably India, cutting right through the heart of Afghanistan's Kandahar province, where the neo-Taliban and assorted Pashtun guerrillas and new generation freedom fighters are, and will continue to be, merrily running rings around NATO.

TAPI's rival is of course the IPI (Iran-Pakistan-India), also know as the "Peace Pipeline," widely derided within the U.S. by Heritage Foundation types, who cannot conceive of India and Pakistan importing gas from Iran. But immense doubts persist about TAPI's supposed output: that depends on the Manila-based Asian Development Bank (ADB), who's paying for the bulk of the project, to know how much gas Turkmenistan can actually offer.

Despite thunderous threats from the Bush administration, nobody in South Asia in fact paid much attention. The U.S. State Dept. is capable of rambling forever on America's "fundamental strategic interest" in Afghanistan without ever making a single reference to the words "oil" or "gas." India and Pakistan will supervise their own leg of pipeline construction. Gazprom and BP are potential bidders for IPI. India anyway cannot wait—and Iran knows it. In 2007, for instance, when global energy consumption rose by 3%, India accounted for a third of the total. Pakistan, for its part, a virtually broke state, could use the $200 million a year in IPI transit fees, not to mention count on a strategic plus regarding India.

Dr. Noor Jehan Panezai, a Parliament member from Western Pakistan, which will be crossed by IPI, did not fail to identify the huge job opportunities: "Indians and Pakistanis will choose our own projects. We have decided that the United States has no business in our problems." This means it was decided months before the inauguration there's no way an Obama presidency would punish allies India and Pakistan—politically or financially—for doing business with Iran. IPI will be an absolutely essential Pipelineistan node in the emerging Asian Energy Security Grid.

As for TAPI, construction should theoretically start in 2010, with gas being supplied by 2015. The government of Afghan President Hamid Karzai, which cannot even provide security for a few streets in central Kabul, engaged in Hollywood-style suspension of disbelief by assuring unsuspecting customers it will not only get rid of millions of land mines blocking TAPI's route, it will get rid of the Taliban themselves.

The new U.S. push for TAPI sent a frantic red alert right to the core of the Canadian government, which is now contemplating the geopolitical nightmare of having its troops, alongside NATO's, protecting a fragile pipeline in a war zone. Canada has committed to keep troops in Afghanistan at least until 2011.

The Canadian Center for Policy Alternatives released a report, *A Pipeline Through a Troubled Land: Afghanistan, Canada and the New Great Energy Game*, written by John Foster, energy economist and former lead economist of PetroCanada, depicting TAPI as turning Afghanistan into "an energy bridge" between Central and South Asia. But Foster is very worried "the quest for 'energy security' risks drawing Canada unwittingly into a new Great Energy Game."

Were investors, perhaps nursed by Afghan opium, to be delirious enough to build such a pipeline—and that's a monumental if—Afghanistan would collect a mere $160 million a year in transit fees. Well, that's maybe not so grim considering it's the equivalent of 50% of Karzai's current annual revenue. The Taliban—and bandits in general—would love to get a piece of the action.

Forget about all that old 2001 "bringing freedom to Afghan women" rhetoric. TAPI's roller-coaster history goes back to the mid-1990s Clinton era, when the Taliban were wined and dined by California-based Unocal—and the Clinton machine. Unocal beat the competition, led by Argentina's Bridas. The negotiations broke down because of money—those pesky transit fees. At the Group of Eight summit in Genoa in July 2001 it was decided the U.S. would take out the Taliban by October; September 11, 2001, accelerated the schedule by a fraction.

One of the first actual fruits of the U.S. bombing of Afghanistan in 2001 was that in December Karzai, then Pakistani President Pervez Musharraf and Turkmenistan's wacky Saparmurad Nyazov (now dead) signed an agreement committing themselves to build TAP (by then known as the Trans-Afghan Pipeline). The Russians decided to wait for their counterpunch, and delivered it in style in September 2006.

Gazprom accepted a 40% price increase demanded by Nyazov for his gas. In return, the Russians got priceless gifts: control of all of Turkmenistan's gas surplus up to 2009; a preference for Russia to tap the new Yolotan gas fields; and Turkmenistan bowing out of any Trans-Caspian pipeline project. Nyazov pledged to supply all his country's gas to Russia.

Thus, dead on arrival, lay TAP, the (invisible) star of the "good" Afghan war, as President Obama sees it. Washington's plan has always been to seduce Nyazov to provide Turkmenistan gas to BTC and then to TAP. This was part of a U.S. grand strategy of a "Greater Central Asia" centered on Afghanistan and India, which now lays practically in tatters. Zbig Brzezinski, of course, would disagree, and may try to convince Obama the world needs a $7.6 billion, 1,600-km steel serpent in a horribly dangerous war zone.

2J. WILL OBAMA GO FOR A RUSSIA/IRAN SPLIT?

Together, Russia and Iran control roughly 20% of world's oil reserves and nearly 50% of the world's gas reserves. Iran is working under the assumption that by 2025 it will become the second-largest gas producer in the world—it is currently behind Russia, the U.S., and Canada—and responsible for up to 10% of the global gas trade, be it in Pipelineistan or as selling LNG.

Iran's momentum of forging an ultra-close partnership with Russia and being open for business with the EU is relentless. In July 2008 Gazprom's CEO, Alexei Miller, was in Tehran agreeing on a "full package of projects" with NIOC. This means direct Russian access to Iran's energy wealth. So what Obama and the EU will face in practice is not only an unstoppable Russian machine controlling the gas flows to Europe; it's nothing less than a Russian-Iranian energy alliance. The neo-con wet dream of a strike on Iran recedes into nothingness.

Iran already exchanges energy with Azerbaijan, Armenia and Turkmenistan. Now it will also connect to Russia's power grid—all the new investment is Russian. This means the Russo-Iranian electricity merger will cover virtually all the demand in Central Asia and the Caucasus.

There's still no way to understand the relative positioning of Iran and the U.S. in relation to Eurasia without considering Iran in 1953 when, as popular opinion in Tehran rules, the country was "taken hostage" by the U.S.

Anglo-Iranian Petroleum—Britain's largest and most profitable holding anywhere in the world—later turned into BP, had taken over the entire Iranian oil industry, with exclusive rights to extract, refine, ship and sell Iranian oil. Iran was paid a pittance in return while Aramco, the Arab American Oil Company, had a 50-50 deal with the House of Saud. Prime Minister Mossadegh had risen to power in 1951 on a nationalist platform. The Iranian parliament voted—unanimously—for the nationalization of Anglo-Iranian.

As former *New York Times* correspondent Stephen Kinzer, author of *All the Shah's Men*, told Amy Goodman, "bear in mind that the oil that fueled England all during the 1920s and '30s and '40s all came from Iran. The standard of living that people in England enjoyed all during that period was due exclusively to Iranian oil. Britain has no oil. Britain has no colonies that have oil. Every factory in England, every car, every truck, every taxi was running on oil from Iran. The Royal Navy, which was projecting British power all over the world ,was fueled 100 percent by oil from Iran."

The British went imperialist over Iran—imposing a crushing economic and naval embargo and refusing to train Iranians to run the oil refinery. They took Mossadegh to the UN and the World Court—arguing that the Iranian oil industry was British private property. It all failed miserably. Mossadegh for his part shut down the British embassy—causing massive unemployment among the spies plotting a coup d'Etat. Then Prime Minister Churchill asked U.S. President Harry Truman to do it. Truman refused.

Finally there was regime change in the U.S. in 1952. Dwight Eisenhower took office. John Foster Dulles, Eisenhower's Secretary of State, was a corporate lawyer. CIA agent Kermit Roosevelt was dispatched to Iran in the summer of 1953—and as legend has it, deposed Mossadegh in just 3 weeks armed with a bag full of money.

Blowback was inevitable—the rise and fall of the Shah, the Islamic Revolution, the Iran-Iraq war, the rise and fall of the Soviet Union in Afghanistan, 9/11, the fall of the Taliban and Saddam, and the reemergence of Iran—the leader of Shi'iteistan—as a regional power.

In 2003, Tehran was ready to talk to Washington, delivering to the Swiss ambassador in Tehran a roll call of items to be negotiated, including the nuclear program, support for Hezbollah and Hamas, and the Beirut Declaration (the Arab world recognizing Israel in exchange for Israel accepting a Palestinian state within 1967 borders). The Bush administration—drunk with neo-con hubris—not only ignored it but actually reprimanded the Swiss ambassador. **Obama now has a unique chance to change the course—whether the negotiating partner is former**

President and uber-pragmatist Rafsanjani or former President Muhammad "dialogue of civilizations" Khatami, before a face-to-face meeting with Supreme Leader Ayatollah Khamenei.

Obama also won't fail to notice that while Washington refuses to talk to Tehran, Russia reaps all the benefits.

Radzhab Safarov, General Director of the Russian Center for Iranian Studies, wrote an essential piece in the small, liberal paper *Vremya Novosti* in August 2008 where he outlined the Russian-Iranian strategic partnership.

After pointing out "the most serious step which the United States and especially Israel fear is hypothetical revision of Russia's foreign policy with regard to Iran," Safarov stresses, "a strategic alliance presuming the signing of a new large-scale military political treaty with Iran could change the entire geopolitical picture of the contemporary world."

Safarov continues: "New allied relations may result in the deployment of at least two military bases in strategic regions of Iran. One military base could be deployed in the north of the country in the Iranian province of Eastern Azerbaijan and the other one in the south, on the Island of Qeshm in the Persian Gulf. Due to the base in Iran's Eastern Azerbaijan Russia would be able to monitor military activities in the Republic of Azerbaijan, Georgia and Turkey and share this information with Iran. The deployment of a military base on the Island of Qeshm would allow Russia to monitor the United States' and NATO's activities in the Persian Gulf zone, Iraq and other Arab states."

Thus, "for the first time ever Russia will have a possibility to stop suspicious vessels and ships and inspect their cargo, which the Americans have been cynically doing in that zone for many decades."

If Iran gets Russian military bases in its territory, it will probably ask for Russia's S-400 SAMs. According to Safarov, "the Iranian leadership paid close attention to reports stating that a Georgian government's secret resolution gave the United States and Israel *carte blanche* to use Georgian territory and local military bases for delivering missile and bomb strikes against Iranian facilities in the event of need. Another neighbor, Turkey, is not only a NATO member, but also a powerful regional opponent and economic rival of Iran. In addition to this, the Republic of Azerbaijan has become the West's key partner on the issue of transportation of Caspian energy resources to world markets. The Iranians are also concerned at Baku's plans to give Western (above all American) capital access to the so-called Azerbaijani sector of the Caspian Sea, which is fraught with new conflicts, because the legal status of the Caspian Sea has not been defined to date. Russia and Iran can also accelerate the process of setting up a cartel of leading gas producers, which journalists have already dubbed the 'gas OPEC'."

There are many other implications to this very close Russo-Iranian strategic partnership—from Russia making a killing by building more nuclear plants in Iran, to Russia lobbying hard with China to finally incorporate Iran as a full member of the SCO. As this might happen by 2010, an Obama presidency has to be prepared for the emergence of a very powerful political-economic-military axis: Russia-China-Iran. That would be the defining moment in the gradual transfer of power from the West to Asia.

One month after the Safarov piece Professor Güner Özkan, a Caucasus expert at the Ankara-based International Strategic Research Organization (ISRO/USAK), writing on *Global Research*, described how the SCO, always insisting on a multipolar world order, was now asserting Russia has an exclusive right to shape its "near abroad."

For Russia, Pipelineistan means de facto control over its 'near abroad'.

Oil and gas are responsible for nearly two-thirds of Russia's exports.Russia can also count on the support of the little-known Collective Security Treaty Organization (CSTO)—a 2002 body that grew out of the Russian-led Collective Security Organization of 1993 and dealt with security involving Russia, Armenia, Belarus, Kyrgyzstan, Kazakhstan, Tajikistan and Uzbekistan. Just like the SCO, the heads of state of the CSTO, in a summit in Moscow, also supported Russia in the Russia-Georgia war and duly blasted the West's "double standards."

The bottom line is that the Russian "near abroad" is more than focused: it won't be looking West anymore, but rather East.

2K. TURKMENBASH

For the Obama presidency, the geopolitical implications of all the twists and turns in the new New Great Game in Eurasia are nothing short of earth-shattering. The Clinton legacy in the Caspian and Central Asia is in tatters. The Bush/neo-con demonization of Russia has been beyond counterproductive: even former Secretaries of State Henry Kissinger and George Shultz have penned op-eds rebuking the Bush administration for its "drift towards confrontation with Russia" and stressing that "isolating Russia is not a sustainable long-range policy."

The U.S.-generated global financial crisis turned remaining U.S. credibility to dust. Russia dominates Pipelineistan, ensuring Central Asia gas flows across Russia's network and not through the Trans-Caspian networks privileged by the U.S. and EU, thus virtually guaranteeing Russia's status as top gas supplier to Europe. No European energy major can match Gazprom. Claude Mandil, former head of the IEA and now advisor to French President Sarkozy on energy issues, told Russian daily *Kommersant*, "There is much oil and gas in Central Asia, but still less than in Russia or Iran." Mandil has always defined relentless U.S. pressure on Europe to isolate Russia as "counter-productive."

Moreover, Russian energy majors are now encroaching over Latin America. Exit U.S. majors ExxonMobil and ConocoPhillips; now Gazprom, LUKoil and TNK-BP have signed lucrative agreements with Venezuela's PDVSA.

But the beauty of Pipelineistan is that the game goes on forever.

Just when Russia thought it had Turkmenistan locked in...

Gas republic Turkmenistan does not hold this denomination for nothing. Its gigantic gas fields have not even been fully explored. When British consultancy firm Gaffney, Cline & Associates (GCA) confirmed in October 2008 that Yoloten-Osman in southeast Turkmenistan were among the world's four largest gas fields, holding as much as a staggering 14 trillion cubic meters and overtaking even the fabulous Dowalatabad field, Turkmenistan instantly became the holder of the world's second-largest gas reserves—way ahead of Iran and only 20% behind of Russia. The earth shook across Russia, China, the EU and the U.S.

Just before he died in December 2006, flamboyant Niyazov had boasted that Turkmenistan held enough reserves to export 150 billion cubic meters of gas annually for the next 250 years. Given his notorious megalomania, nobody took him seriously. But in March 2008 the spectacularly-named Berdimukhamedov ordered an GCA audit to dispel any doubts. After all Turkmenistan has signed contracts to supply Russia with around 50 billion cubic meters annually, China with 40 billion cubic meters and Iran with 8 billion cubic meters.

Turkmenistan and Russia may be playing the definitive Pipelineistan Russian roulette. Turkmenistan raises the stakes non-stop. Up to 2007 Gazprom used to pay $65 for 1,000 cubic meters of gas. Then it had to start paying $100. For the first half of 2008 the price was raised to $130, for the second half it reached $150. Gazprom has to put up with it: without Turkmen gas it cannot export all it needs to Europe, the source of 70% of Gazprom's profits.

According to a Gazprom source quoted by *Kommersant*, the stark fact is that Gazprom, even after the monster 2007 deal whereby it gained control of gas exports from Turkmenistan, Kazakhstan and Uzbekistan as long as it paid them European prices, does not control all of Turkmenistan's gas exports. The new mega-fields are not part of the deal. As *Asia Times'* M.K. Bhadrakumar gleefully put it, "that is proving to be a misconception of Himalayan proportions."

Obama's strategists will endure countless white nights considering that with all that new gas, Turkmenistan by itself would make Nabucco viable— and even possibly defeat Russia's South Stream, fulfilling the U.S. strategic objective of snatching Austria, Italy, Greece and the Balkan and Central European countries from Gazprom's orbit. Washington will not even consider sidelining its Trans-Caspian pipeline dreams. And abandon any hopes of Secretary of State Hillary Clinton complaining about

Turkmenistan's appalling human rights record. Anyway Gazprom can still count on using its virtually unlimited funds—even during the financial crisis—to fend off any Western majors desperately trying to curry favors in Ashgabat.

2L. China Wins, Again

While U.S. pragmatists and Cold Warriors may remain obsessed with fighting the Russia bear on the Caspian, the Caucasus and the steppes of Central Asia, once again the winner in this game between Russia and the U.S.—and the EU—via Turkmenistan may in fact be China.

Turkmenistan will have to deliver up to 40 billion cubic meters of gas annually to China via the $2.6 billion, fully Chinese-financed Central Asia-China node of Pipelineistan. And China is also partnering with local Kazakhs and Uzbek companies in its own Pipelineistan push.

The Central Asians love it because China carries absolutely no local imperial baggage—unlike Russia and the U.S.—and it will never be involved in peddling respect for human rights or any sort of color-coded revolution.

China's deft energy diplomacy game plan is the opposite of the U.S.—offering lucrative deals and partnering with Russia to boost Turkmen gas production. No antagonism—as befits SCOP partners. Thus the obligatory *People's Daily* editorials extolling the "great success" of Russia's Central Asia diplomacy. More typical of the Pipelineistan Great Game is convoluted stuff such as this pearl from Kazakh Foreign Minister Marat Tazhin: "Our relationship with Russia, I can formulate, is just excellent. We have very good political relations. Russia is our strategic partner. At the same time, I should underline that our relationship with the United States has a stable, strategic character."

As for the very influential head of the CIS committee of the Russian Parliament, Vadim Gustov, he sees an "oil alliance" between Russia and Kazakhstan as the basis for a proposed EuroAsian Economic Community space. Now that would be a certified spoiler to Washington's dreams.

2M. MEET THE GAS OPEC

When Gazprom reached its new status of one and only buyer of Turkmen gas—before the GCA audit of the monster Turkmen fields—Russia seemed to be on its way to set prices in the world gas market. *China Daily* raved about it, headlining "Russia might turn its eyes from the Western countries to the Asia-Pacific region." In the Kremlin's grand strategy of forging a new geopolitics of energy security, the idea of a "gas cartel"—always vehemently opposed by the EU—was back in business, even tough Washington had already warned that it would go out guns blazing against any countries in a "gas cartel."

By October 2008 Russia and Iran finally decided to act. Russia, Iran and Qatar—which among them control 60% of the world's gas reserves—went on the record to acknowledge the birth of a gas OPEC. Alexei Miller, chairman of Russia's Gazprom, said they were forming a "big gas troika" and warned—even before the latest IEA report—the era of cheap hydrocarbons had come to an end.

Miller stressed, "We are united by the world's largest gas reserves, common strategic interests and, which is of great importance, high cooperation potential in tripartite projects"—a reference to a technical committee already charged of studying everything from geological exploration to marketing. A gas OPEC would be eventually joined by Turkmenistan, Venezuela, Bolivia, Algeria—and would imprint a very powerful mark on the Obama presidency, certainly speeding up research in wind and an array of renewable energy alternatives.

The European Commission predictably reacted with a mix of anger and fury, stressing, "energy supplies have to be sold in a free market." For most Europeans the perception remains that Russia—and in a smaller scale Iran—use energy as a political weapon. A gas cartel would make both Russia and Iran even more powerful. LNG could be traded as a commodity—just as oil.

LNG is bound to become a star of the post-crisis global economy—capturing 38% of the gas market before 2020. LNG is 600 times less voluminous than natural gas and its transportation—by cryogenic ships—

and storage are cheaper and more flexible (although the prospect of the explosion of an LNG tanker is daunting and will raise environmental concerns). Winners will include, apart from the "troika," Indonesia, Malaysia, Nigeria and Trinidad-Tobago.

Konstantin Batunin, an analyst with Moscow's Alfa Bank, dampened expectations about the gas OPEC, saying "My take is that it is just a commitment to create something in the future." Russia has always avoided using the term "cartel." But the Iranian leadership preferred to reach for the jugular, stressing this was the most significant step toward the formation of a gas OPEC since Supreme Leader Ayatollah Khamenei came up with the idea in January 2007.

2N. WILL NATO EVER GIVE UP?

In early October 2008 NATO Defense ministers got together in Budapest to authorize nothing less than full spectrum dominance, or a "war on terror" hit, on the Indian Ocean (which is a long way indeed from the North Atlantic). NATO got the go ahead to go all the way against peasant poppy growers and drug warlords in the "good" Afghan war and go all the way against pirates in the Indian Ocean—ostensibly to "protect" World Food Program ships carrying famine relief for Somalia, which had allegedly landed the request.

NATO's Supreme Allied Commander in Europe, General John Craddock, didn't even disguise NATO's self-ascribed role of global cop: "The threat of piracy is real and growing in many parts of the world today, and this response is a good illustration of NATO's ability to adapt quickly to new security challenges."

NATO's virtually open-ended deployment in the Indian Ocean—with Indian blessing—is a formidable new geostrategic challenge to Asia. For China, which imports armies of containers loaded with oil via the Indian Ocean, this is a supreme matter of national security. China was silent. But SCO partner Russia responded on the spot; also claiming to attend a request from the government of Somalia, a missile frigate from Russia's Baltic fleet—the timely named *Neustrashimy* [Fearless]—was dispatched to the Indian Ocean to reportedly "fight piracy off Somalia's coast." Russia is ready to play NATO's game and also go on "war on terror" mode in the Indian Ocean.

Nobody really knows how NATO—or India, or Russia—high seas patrolling falls in accordance with international law. NATO insists it is under orders from pliable UN secretary-general Ban Ki-moon, who does not bat an eye without Washington's approval.

Formally becoming operational on October 1, 2008, AFRICOM signaled the start of the Pentagon's new game in Africa, It was met with extreme suspicion by almost all African governments, who identify it for what it is: Liquid War—or the "war on terror" legitimizing a mad U.S. scramble for natural resources against emerging China and India, including expanded nodes of Pipelineistan. African resistance to AFRICOM was so fierce that the HQ had to be set up in Stuttgart, with liaison officers posted at U.S. embassies across the continent.

AFRICOM and NATO will inevitably link up—as confirmed by U.S. officials on the record. Translation—in Beijing and Moscow: NATO will have to be counteracted as the U.S. "global" security arm from Africa and the Middle East to the Indian Ocean.

NATO's conquest of the Indian Ocean relies not only on India (the Indian navy would love nothing better than to get full access to top U.S. defense technology), but on Sri Lanka (which overlooks the ultra-strategic sea lanes connecting the Persian Gulf and the Strait of Malacca) and Singapore (Singapore performs the role of a reliable Cold War ally aircraft carrier overlooking the equally ultra-strategic Strait of Malacca). For all of it to fall into place presupposes the end of the Tamil Tiger guerrillas.

The master plan is for NATO—that is, the U.S. and Europe, plus India—to ultimately monitor China. "Pirates" are just an excuse. This has to do with a fabulous wealth of natural gas and possibly oil, plus uranium, iron ore, tin, gypsum, bauxite, copper and salt.

The mad scramble for African energy and natural resources provides the rationale behind the Bush administration, in its death throes, drafting a

UN Security Council resolution, later approved, giving that usual suspect, the "international community," a mandate to "hunt down" alleged pirates even inside Somali territory and airspace. By the end of 2008, what passed for a "government" in Somalia, thanks to a Bush-administration-inspired 2006 invasion, was a disgraced coalition of CIA-financed warlords and invading Ethiopian thugs controlling a few city blocks of territory. The key financial supporters of the pirate gangs happen to be directly linked to the collapsing Western-backed "government."

Somalia—on a pure "war on terror" register—elicits striking parallels with Afghanistan. Everyone and his neighbor—except, of course, Pentagon "analysts"—knew Somalia historically had never embraced radical Saudi Wahhabism. U.S. proxy Ethiopia—by indiscriminately bombing civilians—may have driven Islamists out of power in Mogadishu, but they went into exile and radical Islam outfits, with huge popular appeal, ended up controlling southern Somalia. The puppet government in Mogadishu is a Somali version of Karzai's in Afghanistan: installed by a foreign invasion and corrupted to the core. Now comes the Pakistani tribal areas gambit— Somalia converted into a giant Fallujah under U.S. and NATO-ordered "precision strikes."

20. AN OBAMA/MEDVEDEV COUPLE?

On November 15, 2008, during a tense G-20 summit in Washington to discuss the global financial crisis, the question on everyone's lips was "Where is Carla?" Well, in the end stunning Carla Bruni-Sarkozy was in New York, waiting for his French presidential husband—who had proposed the summit in the first place—to get rid of a gray, rainy day in Washington and join her for some Big Apple fun and games.

Besides Carla-watching, the next best game in town had to be Russian President Dmitry Medvedev. Speaking at the historic Washington Club in a Council on Foreign Relations meeting moderated by former Secretary of State Madeleine Albright, Medvedev summed up the Bush administration's legacy: "On many stances we can't find common ground ... It's a deplorable fact, but that is life."

Medvedev suggested with Obama things might—might—be different. Provided, of course, there were no NATO shenanigans in place—such as an Obama administration insisting Europe had to be defended from "rogue missiles" launched by Iran.

The day after Obama's confirmation victory on November 4, Medvedev had been on Russian TV on a State of the Nation speech vowing to prevent any U.S. deployment of anti-missile batteries or radars on any territory of former Warsaw Pact members. Medvedev also accused the U.S. of starting the war in Georgia and throwing the global economy in disarray by having provoked a monster financial crisis.

Medvedev told his exclusive Washington audience that for Russia, as had been stressed previously, NATO should be replaced—or expanded to a trans-European security pact including Russia and other former Soviet republics. Up to the beginning of his presidency Obama remained silent on missile defense in Central Europe. Medvedev anyway had not given up on what he stressed in his Washington speech—cautious optimism: "In my state of the nation address I mentioned that Russia has no anti-Americanism."

Only a few days after Medvedev's Washington trip Igor Panarin, a professor at the Diplomatic Academy of the Russian Ministry of Foreign Affairs, and author of several books on information warfare, said in an interview with daily *Izvestia*, regarding U.S. global domination: "It is already collapsing .... Now what we will see is a change in the regulatory system on a global financial scale: America will no longer be the world's financial regulator."

Panarin had made his first predictions about the U.S. economy in Australia 10 years ago—when the U.S. economy was booming. He did not fail to mention "divisions among the [U.S.] elite, which have become clear in these crisis conditions." When asked who would replace the U.S. in regulating world markets, he didn't blink: "Two countries could assume this role: China, with its vast reserves, and Russia, which could play the role of a regulator in Eurasia."

With this background of inexorable U.S. decline and emerging multipolarity, a few days later Dmitry Medvedev went to India—not to simply sell gas, like the Iranians, but to propose a wide-ranging trilateral partnership among Russia, China and India. He arrived in India in the immediate aftermath of the terror strike on Mumbai. The Indian elite was as stunned by the attack as by Medvedev's proposal.

The Russo-Indian joint declaration duly stressed "multilateral dialogue," "newly emerging multipolarity" and "collective leadership."

From Medvedev's point of view it was clear: Russia wants India much closer to the SCO ("more constructive participation and contribution," in official terms) and a decisive rapprochement between India and China.

The *entente cordiale* is at full speed. As much as India is in favor of Russia joining the Asia-Europe (ASEM) meetings and the East Asia summit mechanisms, Russia supports India as a permanent member in an expanded UN Security Council.

But what was most striking was the common call for a "coherent and a united international commitment" to Afghanistan. In practice, this is a devastating indictment of the "war of terror." And then the clincher: both Russia and India proposing an international conference in the framework of the SCO, with all members and observers (these include, of course, Iran and Pakistan). That envelops an immense geostrategic development: the SCO—and not NATO—deciding the future of Afghanistan. The trillion-dollar question is how the Obama presidency's Afghan strategy will deal with it.

So India may now be officially aligned with Russia, China and Iran—and thus with the SCO—in identifying the Afghan tragedy as an Asian problem. India is more than aware that Afghanistan is a potential, crucial and profitable bridge between South Asia and Central Asia. The loser in this case would be the long-running Clinton-Bush "Great Central Asia" strategy that has always spurned the SCO in Central Asia by pushing India against both Russia and China.

For all his government's corruption and incompetence, Karzai now has every reason to cooperate with the SCO—where all the major powers surrounding Afghanistan such as Russia, China, India and Iran are involved. Pakistan, as a SCO observer, should also be on board. So far, the Bush administration had been privileging a Turkish mediation between Afghanistan and Pakistan. And the SCO does not believe in U.S.-sponsored, Saudi-mediated talks with "moderate" Taliban. India, Russia and Iran—which all supported the Northern Alliance from 1996 to 2001—dismiss differences between "good" or "bad" Taliban, only recognizing "rank-and-file Taliban members who are not tainted by military crimes."

Now it's up to the Obama presidency to make its move. India seems to have realized that the SCO is part of the solution for Afghanistan—and that it won't be Obama's proposed surge that will solve the Afghan tragedy. Russia and the SCO insist, "the situation in Afghanistan cannot be fixed by solely military means," and security must be coupled with real, strong measures to impel Afghanistan's socio-economic revival.

And so we have come full circle. The SCO was founded in June 2001, among other reasons, as a security belt around Afghanistan. The SCO is now way beyond a mere "energy club" in Asia. The question of who will "win" Afghanistan—NATO or SCO—may well be the defining foreign policy question of the Obama presidency.

It's wishful thinking to believe U.S. ruling elites will simply abandon the new New Great Game in Eurasia and thus leave Russia to freely play with its near abroad from the Caucasus and Central Asia and a power coalition emerge to the exclusion of the U.S. If not India, both Russia and Iran, as well as China, are in yellow-to-red Liquid War alert: their strategists have fully identified the "war on terror" as just a cover for the U.S. to secure permanent bases in the Hindu Kush and the Pamirs, in the Central Asian steppes, and in the Caucasus.

If Obama's Eurasian policy reveals itself to be Bush 3, Russia already has a perfect short-term counterpunch in the wings: it will sell the S-300 missile defense system—the stuff of NATO nightmares—to Iran. The S-300 is an ultra high-tech surface-to-air missile system capable of intercepting no less than 100 ballistic missiles or jet fighters at once, be it at low or high altitude, within a range of over 150 km.

In terms of preventing any possibility of the strengthening of the SCO, it's fair to expect the Obama presidency to exploit every single fissure between China and India, China and Russia, India and Pakistan, Iran and Pakistan and Russia and Pakistan: this is textbook British imperial "divide and rule"—although "ruling" in this case is more than elusive: it would mean in practical terms the U.S. killing the SCO-proposed international conference on Afghanistan.

As my *Asia Times* colleague, Indian ambassador M K Bhadrakumar, has indelibly put it: "The million-dollar question is Obama's sincerity. If he genuinely wants to end the bloodshed and the suffering in Afghanistan, tackle terrorism effectively and enduringly, as well as stabilize Afghanistan and secure South Asia as a stable region, he has to make a definitive choice. All he needs to do is to feel disgusted with the 'collateral damage' that the great game is causing to the human condition, and seek an inclusive Afghan settlement in terms of the imperatives of regional security and stability. Such a break will be consistent with what he claims his sense of values to be. The existential choice is whether he will break with the past out of principle." That would mean Obama confronting head on the industrial-military complex, the maze of national security agencies, Big Oil and Washington's irremovable Cold War mentality.

So this, in a nutshell is the Liquid War landscape the Obama presidency will inherit. The SCO uniting China, Russia and Central Asia with Iran and in the long run with India. Solidification of the Asian Security Energy Grid. A leading Russia role in Pipelineistan. It's never enough to stress that absolutely none of this has anything to do with Zbig Brzezinski's dream of the U.S. as the dominant power in Eurasia.

How Obama will position himself regarding this multipolarity? As the inestimable David Harvey told me at his office in New York in the summer of 2008, before the financial crisis: Ultra-imperialism, "at least the U.S. version of it," is over.

So what next? "The question on the agenda is 'Can there be a collective version of it, in which the Europeans, in alliance with North America, in alliance with Japan, decide to collectively stabilize the world using U.S. military power, which is still dominant at least from 30,000 feet up, not so much on the ground; if they can use U.S. military power and at the same time use their collective economic power we might see a kind of collective kind of imperialism."

Obama, in this scenario, would be just a cog in the mechanism. Way before the election, and even before the apotheosis of the August 2008 Democratic convention in Denver, Harvey was already warning about the enormous expectations Obama was rising; yet he was essentially a "very conservative figure," surrounded by center-right advisers. In sum: "A gentler face of neoliberal imperialism."

The die is now cast, and Harvey himself hinted what might happen: "Social and collective movements in this country, and when they do erupt, can erupt very strongly, that may well be a strong reaction to his passivity, if he is passive."

And that brought Harvey to the question the whole planet must answer: "Have we reached the limits of a capitalist social order? Capitalism, since its very inception, has been dedicated to a compound rate of growth. When capitalism was twenty square miles around Manchester, that's different from a compound rate of growth of global capitalism, with China, Russia, India, Brazil, as well as the traditional powers all involved. A compound rate of growth of where we are now, for the next hundred years, that would be an astonishing thing to accomplish. So there's gonna be a real transformation in the way the global economy works over the next twenty years. I don't believe that any particular group of people in the world will be hegemonic or dominant. It will be a multipolar world, but also there will be a lot of agitation over 'this is not the kind of world we want to live in', environmentally, socially and politically."

SELECTED BIBLIOGRAPHY

Ali, Tariq. *The Duel: Pakistan on the Flight Path of American Power.* Scribner, New York, 2008.

Bauman, Zygmunt. *Liquid Fear.* Polity Press, Cambridge, 2006.

Beck, Ulrich. Conditio Humana: *Il Rischio Nell'Età Globale.* Laterza, Roma, 2008.

Brzezinski, Zbigniew. *The Grand Chessboard: American Primacy and the Geostrategic Imperatives.* Basic Books, New York, 1997.

Brzezinski, Zbigniew; Scowcroft, Brent; Ignatius, David. America and the World: *Conversations on the Future of American Foreign Policy.* Basic Books, New York, 2008.

Cusset, François. *French Theory: How Foucault, Derrida, Deleuze, & Co. Transformed the Intellectual Life of the United States.* University of Minnesota Press, Minneapolis, 2008.

Engelhardt, Tom, editor. *The World According to Tomdispatch: America and the Age of Empire.* Verso, New York, 2008.

Escobar, Pepe. *Globalistan: How the Globalized World is Dissolving into Liquid War.* Nimble Books, Ann Arbor, 2007.

Gray, John. *Black Mass:Apocalyptic Religion and the Death of Utopia.* Allen Lane, London, 2007.

Harvey, David. *A Brief History of Neoliberalism.* Oxford University Press, 2007.

Hobsbawm, Eric. *On Empire: America, War, and Global Supremacy.* Pantheon Books, New York, 2008.

Johnson, Chalmers. *The Sorrows of Empire: Militarism, Secrecy, and the End of the Republic.* Metropolitan Books, New York, 2004.

Klare, Michael T. *Rising Powers, Shrinking Planet: The New Geopolitics of Energy*. Metropolitan Books, New York, 2008.

Marx, Karl; Engels, Friedrich. *The Communist Manifesto*. Introduction by David Harvey. Pluto Press, London, 2008.

Negri, Antonio. *Goodbye Mister Socialism*. Seuil, Paris, 2007.

Rodríguez Garavito, César; Barret, Patrick S.; Chavez, Daniel, editors. *La Nueva Izquierda en América Latina*. Grupo Norma, Buenos Aires, 2005.

Roy, Olivier. *The Politics of Chaos in the Middle East*. Columbia University Press, New York, 2008.

Schwartz, Michael. *War Without End: The Iraq War in Context*. Haymarket, New York, 2008.

Todd, Emmanuel. *Après l'Empire*. Gallimard, Paris, 2002.

Turse, Nick. *The Complex: How the Military Invades our Everyday Lives*. Metropolitan Books, New York, 2008.

Zizek, Slavoj. *Iraq: The Borrowed Kettle*. Verso, New York, 2005.

Selected Webroll

Al Jazeera

AlterNet

Antiwar.com

Asia Times Online

Bolpress.com

China Daily

China Digital Times

Common Dreams

Council on Foreign Relations

Counterpunch

Courrier International

Daily Kos

DARPA

Dawn

Eschaton

EUobserver.com

Ferghana.ru

Fernand Braudel Center

Firedoglake

Foreign Policy in Focus

FT.com

GlobalResearch.ca

Guardian Unlimited

Independent Online

Information Clearing House

Informed Comment/Juan Cole

Iran Daily

Irna

Kommersant

La Repubblica

Le Monde Diplomatique

Le Monde.fr

MediaBite

Nezavissimaya Gazeta

Open Source Center

Outlook India

Página 12

Peyamner News Agency

Politico.com

Press TV

RealClearPolitics

Rebelión

RGE Monitor

RIA Novosti

Rue89

Russia Today

Spiegel Online

Talking Points Memo

The Huffington Post

The Nation

The News International

The Raw Story

The Real News

The Washington Note

Think Progress

Tomdispatch

Truthdig

Truthout

Venezuelanalysis.com

Vremya Novosti

WhatReallyHappened.com

PRAISE FOR *GLOBALISTAN*

This marvelous book by Pepe Escobar, the well-known "Roving Eye" of *Asia Times Online*, ought to be placed on the desk of every member of the U.S. Congress, as well as British Parliament members and any others who are debating placing their troops in far-flung remote areas of the world to "make the world safe for Globalistan."

Escobar is at his inimitable best in his personal narratives, with his keen eye for the absurdities of the globalizing world, the contrast between obscenely wealthy and dirt poor. It is no simple description, however. He has not merely gone to Iraq or Afghanistan as a journalist embedded in to a NATO fighting unit to report the filtered perceptions allowed reporters in this bizarre new form of controlled journalism. Escobar gets out of the jeep, wanders off the beaten paths, into the villages, talks with the rich, the poor, the young, the old, the scholars, the tradesmen. The result is in the best tradition of a Peter Schall-Latour or John Gunther, the famous political traveler of the 1940's.

Yet this book should not be mistaken for a travelogue through the mysterious regions of Eurasia or Latin America. It is a rich, political history of our time.

Escobar manages to capture the absurd element of what he appropriately names "Jihad Inc." as a Made in America phenomenon emerging from the ill-considered experiment in the early 1980's by a part of US intelligence to unleash the force of Islamic believers against the Soviet Union in Afghanistan: "Jihad Inc is an American invention, along with associate executive directors Saudi Arabia, Egypt and Pakistan. It was a US strategy in USSR-invaded Afgjhanistan in the 1980's—"Let's launch one billion Muslims against the Evil Empire!"—that catapulted jihad to the forefront of political Islam. Zia ul-Haq, the Pakistani dictator, supported by billions of dollars, could not pass up the opportunity to launch a true, pan-Islamic jihad against Russian infidels. Wahhabi Saudi Arabia also jumped at the golden opportunity to spread its rigid interpretation of Islam. In 1985 Ronald Reagan described the Afghan jihadis visiting him at the White House as the 'moral equivalent of America's founding fathers.' Even at the time Whitney Houston-fan Osama bin Laden would frown if landed in the same corner of lower Paradise in the company of Thomas Jefferson. The Looney Tunes element of it all is deliriously funny—if it was not tragic. First the US pitted political Islam against communism. Then communism died. Now it's the US against political Islam. A historical 'what if' perfectly allows us to think that were the Cold War still on, everyone would still be watching the same movie ..." (p.92).

The writer manages to mix his unique wealth of personal experiences as a global journalist talking, listening, observing, with that of a serious student of culture and history. Another brief excerpt is useful: "But then, around mid-2004, Islamic scholars from Morocco to Malaysia started to finally legitimize al Qaeda as a Muqadamaul Jaish—in fact a revolutionary vanguard. This totally Western concept was absolutely unheard of in Islam—well, at least until the symbolically-charged spring of 2003 when Baghdad was 'liberated' by George W. Bush's Christian armies. The concept of revolutionary vanguard simply does not exist in Islam. Before Hezbollah surged to the fore in the summer of 2006, al Qaeda's internat ionalism might conceive of merging with some radical strands of the only other global protest movement: the alter-globalization, anti-imperlialism brigade ... As much as al Qaeda's only strategic goal is trapping the US, Washington helped al Qaeda by trapping itself in Iraq and in still another, dangerous form of hubris, George W. Bush's Greater Middle East." (pp.100-101).

What is most compelling is the unpretentious manner in which Pepe Escobar sifts through the incredibly complex historically-rooted strands of Islamic history and political geography to clarify the implications of the historical fault-line cutting through Islam, that between Shiite and Sunni and all its manifold complexities. It makes starkly clear how Washington and the pro-war Pentagon hawks are playing with a fire that has the potential to ignite a conflagration not even the Pentagon's Smart Bombs, Full Spectrum Dominance, Net-Centric warfare methods, its Revolution in Military Affairs, laser-guided bombs or deadly chemical weapons would be able to control. Iraq today should serve as ample warming, were anyone in Washington even dimly aware.

On another front in today's "war against the Axis of Evil": "The only reason Afghanistan matters in the (Bush Administration's) Long War worldview remains the same one when the Taliban rose to power: as a transit corridor for (Turkmenistan-Afghanistan-Pakistan pipeline) TAP from Turkmenistan to Baluchistan and eventually to India...The only way for TAP to be profitable is with India as a final destination—and Delhi knows its best bet for natural gas is from Iran, and the second best from Qatar. Hamad Karzai wants TAP by all means—not TAP itself but the badly needed US$300 million a year he could collect in transit fees. In Pakistan the independent Baluchistan Liberation Army would certainly raise some hell to get a piece of the action. The Taliban also have TAP on their sights—but for more ballistic motives ... "(p.168).

Escobar manages to capture the impact of the War on Terrorism as it hits the so-called Islamic street: "The Bush Administration may have demonized [Osama bin Laden] as the Prince of Darkness in a 24/7 planetary soap. But for millions of urban, radicalized, dirt-poor seething in anger in an immense Islamic slum nebula, Osama is comparable to El Comandante Fidel in 1959 Cuba—a true mass hero. Destitute Arab brothers know there are no more heroes rising from the desert like Muhammad in the 7th Century, so for them Osama became the remixed version of the Holy Prophet—the media-savvy Warrior Prophet ... He knows how to tweak the financial markets. And of course he knows everything about Globalistan. No wonder. People from the bin Laden clan are bedouin fishermen from the Hadramut region. They have been 'global' since time immemorial ...'" (p.107).

That's the point. The book illustrates that in some 340 pages of invaluable mixture between personal anecdote and relevant history. The central conclusion the reader is left with is the futility and the unbelievable arrogance of those who believe they can "put into play" forces such as Islam to further their own geopolitical agenda of domination and "pre-emptive" hegemony. It's a 'must read.'

F. William Engdahl, author of A Century of War: Anglo-American Oil Politics and the New World Order, Pluto Press, and Seeds of

Destruction: The Hidden Agenda of Genetic Manipulation,
Global Research.

CPSIA information can be obtained at www.ICGtesting.com
Printed in the USA
BVOW040202060513

319959BV00003B/10/P